Latino Communities

Emerging Voices

Political, Social, Cultural, and Legal Issues

Edited by
Antoinette Sedillo Lopez
University of New Mexico

A ROUTLEDGE SERIES

LATINO COMMUNITIES: EMERGING VOICES

Antoinette Sedillo Lopez, *General Editor*

CARIBBEAN SPANISH IN THE METROPOLIS

Spanish Language among Cubans, Dominicans, and Puerto Ricans in the New York City Area

Edwin M. Lamboy

Routledge
Taylor & Francis Group

LONDON AND NEW YORK

Published in 2004 by

Routledge
Taylor and Francis Group
711 Third Avenue
New York, NY 10017

Routledge
Taylor and Francis Group
2 Park Square
Milton Park, Abingdon
Oxon OX14 4RN

Library of Congress Cataloging-in-Publication Data
    Lamboy, Edwin M., 1967–
        Caribbean Spanish in the Metropolis : Spanish Language among Cubans,
    Dominicans, and Puerto Ricans in the New York City Area / Edwin M. Lamboy.
        p. cm.—(Latino communities)
    Includes bibliographical references and index.
    ISBN 0-415-94925-4 (hardback : alk. paper)
        1. Spanish language—Dialects—New York (State)—New York. 2. Spanish
    language—Dialects—Caribbean. 3. Bilingualism—New York (State)—New York.
    4. Spanish language—Dialects—Phonetics. I. Title. II. Series.

        PC4829.N44L36 2004
        467.'97471—dc22   2004005120

    ISBN 13: 978-0-415-64639-0 (pbk)

Contents

List of Tables and Figures

Acknowledgments

This study is dedicated to three very important persons in my life: my mother, who taught me the value of sacrifice; my grandfather, the male role model who taught me the value of honor; and the love of my life, who teaches me every single day the value of everything else that merits value in life.

The most sincere thanks to all my Penn State professors: John R. Gutiérrez, William Glass, Ana Teresa Pérez-Leroux, Donna Rogers, Lisa Reed, Jorge Guitart, and Margaret Lyday. You showed me a new world, one I had no idea existed.

To the wonderful mentors and friends who gave me valuable comments, suggestions, and encouragement for this project: Marie Gillette, John R. Gutiérrez, José R. Fernández, Nancy Landale, Sal Oropesa, and Rafael Salaberry.

Finally, thanks to the wonderful people I got to meet, talk to, and interview. You make me proud to be Latino like you. Keep on fighting!

Chapter One
Introduction

The Spanish language has been present in the United States since this nation began its formation. The imperialistic nature of Spanish politics during the fifteenth, sixteenth, and seventeenth centuries motivated many conquerors and explorers such as Juan Ponce de Leon, Panfilo de Narvaez, Alonso de Pineda, and Juan Rodríguez Cabrillo to set their expansionist goals on the land northwest of the Caribbean islands. With their view came their language, and as they were able to create settlements and colonies, Spanish represented the vehicle that would guarantee communication with the official government and among themselves for centuries. The Spanish language and culture became a part of the people and territories that had been explored and colonized. Later, the incorporation of Mexican territories into the union of states in 1848, and the immigration waves of the 1900s enhanced the presence of the Spanish language in the United States.

Despite movements toward the imposition of English through educational and political measures (e.g., US English, English only), Spanish has remained remarkably strong. It is the second-most-spoken language in the United States, with approximately 28 million speakers. In fact, it is common to hear more Spanish than English in Spanish-speaking areas of the larger cities of the United States. Some of these cities are Miami, where more than half of the population is of Hispanic/Latino descent and where bilingualism is viewed as an asset; and Los Angeles, which after Mexico City is the largest Spanish-speaking city in the world. Moreover, the United States may be considered the fourth largest Spanish-speaking country in the world, surpassed only by Mexico, Spain, and Argentina (Elías-Olivares et al. 1985, 1). The importance of Spanish in the United States is expected to grow, since it is estimated that Hispanics/Latinos will soon be the largest ethnic minority group (Bailey 1983, 7), and they will probably constitute one-fourth of the entire population of this country within a century (Y. R. Solé 1990, 36).

Research on the Spanish language in the United States began during the first decade of the 1900s with Espinosa's (1909, cited in Zentella 1990a, 152) brilliant description of New Mexican Spanish. This trend gained popularity, however, in the 1970s, partly because of the tradition created by other scholars at the University of New Mexico. As Zentella states (1990a, 152–153), these pioneer studies focused on the Mexican and Puerto Rican populations, with an emphasis on describing how their speech deviated from the Castillian linguistic norm. Later studies included in collections edited during the 1980s and 1990s (Amastae and Elías-Olivares 1983; Elías-Olivares et al. 1985; Bergen 1990; Klee and Ramos 1991; Roca and Lipski 1993; Silva-Corvalán 1994, 1995; Roca and Jensen 1996) shifted their attention toward educational, sociological, psychological, and legal issues. Although the tradition has been kept alive, this field of study has failed to incorporate all the Spanish varieties of speakers currently living in this land—particularly the Cuban, Dominican, and Puerto Rican varieties—, thus painting a fragmentary picture of the linguistic situation of Hispanics/Latinos in this country.

NEED FOR THE STUDY

A number of studies of Spanish in the United States have been completed in the last thirty years. These studies have reported on linguistic, sociolinguistic, attitudinal, and ethnographic aspects of several communities. Research has been concerned primarily with the levels of maintenance and shift, social functions, and specific factors that produce one or another linguistic outcome in certain Hispanic populations. Some of these studies are Attinasi 1979; Elerik 1980; Guitart 1982b, 1996; Gutiérrez 1990; Jacobson 1982; Labov and Pedraza 1971; Ocampo 1990; Padilla and Lindholm 1982; Pfaff 1982; Poplack 1982; Pousada and Poplack 1982; Sobin 1980; Valdés 1982; Wolfram 1971; and Zentella 1982, among others.

This study, however, takes a new approach in an attempt to consider several issues that have yet to be treated in combination. First of all, it deals with data collected from speakers of three Spanish dialects: Cuban, Dominican, and Puerto Rican. The rationale for considering these three groups lies in that it allows for generalizations about Caribbean speakers of Spanish and Caribbean Spanish in a common area, that is, New York City. Secondly, very few studies have paid close attention to the linguistic phenomena that characterize second generation speakers of a given language. As I will discuss later, this generation represents an intermediate stage between absolute or almost absolute usage of the mother tongue and the dominant language, with various degrees of performance ability for both languages in each stage. Furthermore, the literature lacks studies designed to investigate and describe the maintenance of phonetic features among speakers of particular dialects of Spanish, and their capacity to "reproduce" phono-phonetic features of the dialect spoken by the older generation while being in a language (and dialect) contact situation. In particular, this study looks at the issue of maintenance of features among second generation speakers of Cuban, Dominican, and Puerto Rican Spanish in the New York City area, and compares their realization of specific phonemes to that of first generation speakers. In sum, this study encompasses ethnic, regional, dialectal, and demographic characteristics.

ETHNICITY AND IMMIGRATION

The ethnicity criterion, as it relates to the linguistic criterion, plays an important role in this research. The literature about Spanish in the United States includes an ample array of studies on Mexican American and Chicano speech because this is the largest group of Hispanics/Latinos in this country. There is also a substantial number of studies on Cuban and Puerto Rican speech. Dominican speech in the United States, however, has not been deeply explored, in part because this is a group with a relatively recent immigration pattern. But the number of Dominicans in New York City and other East Coast cities has increased dramatically in the last decade. This demographic increase provides a good opportunity to incorporate this group into the tradition of study of Spanish in the United States. The analysis of representative data from the three groups mentioned before provides an interesting perspective of both inter- and intragroup tendencies.

Each ethnic group has followed a clear pattern of immigration into this area. Cubans have settled in cities across the Hudson River such as West New York, Hoboken, and Jersey City; Dominicans are concentrated in the Washington Heights section of Manhattan; and Puerto Ricans in the well-known community of El Barrio.

GENERATIONS

Why concentrate on second generation speakers of these Spanish varieties? Why is it important to compare them to the first generation of speakers? There has been considerable interest in the second generation from a sociological point of view. The immigration experience and the acculturation that commonly results from the experience have been the primary focus of attention. Although some studies have touched on the linguistic issues that affect this sector of the United States population, neither has taken into consideration the linguistic features considered in this study nor focused on the three specific groups mentioned above. This interest is supported by the fact that the real linguistic effects of English over a subordinate language occur in the second generation (Veltman 1988, cited in Oropesa and Landale 1997, 430). As Oropesa and Landale say (1997, 448), "the situation of the second generation is pivotal because it indicates the trajectories that succeeding generations will take from the immigrant experience." In other words, the study of the second generation can provide insights into the effects of integration and assimilation of immigrants within and between generations, as Jensen and Chitose suggest (1994, 715).

DIALECTS

Most of the studies cited in the next chapter provide information on the status of Spanish in the United States, but very few of them deal with those linguistic traits that distinguish the various dialects. Despite the fact that the three Caribbean Spanish dialects in question share a definite set of phono-phonetic characteristics that catalogue them as 'radical' dialects because of the tendency of their speakers to delete or neutralize sounds in syllable-final position, among other things (Guitart 1982a), they also have a subset of features that distinguishes one from the other.

It is equally necessary to explore whether or not each ethnic group shows generational differences. For instance, even though Cuban Americans in Miami have a high Spanish retention rate, we do not know the exact characteristics of their speech. In addition, it is unknown whether the speech of these Cubans differs from the speech of other Cubans with whom they have had contact, or moreover, if it differs from typical Cuban speech as described in the literature. Sánchez (1982) is one of the only studies that comes close to this issue, but her observations are exclusively about Chicano Spanish in the Southwest. Thus, one of the goals of the present study is to describe the qualities of the speech of second generation speakers of the three varieties of Spanish in terms of those phono-phonetic features that make each variety unique and distinct.

PROCEDURE

The database used in this study consists of information gathered in three successive phases, and will be delineated in greater detail in chapter three. The first phase involved the selection of subjects, twenty Dominicans and twenty Puerto Ricans—ten from the first generation and ten from the second generation—and eighteen Cubans—ten from the first generation and eight from the second generation—for a total of fifty-eight subjects. The criterion utilized to determine the generation of the individual was place of birth, based partly on the conclusions presented by Oropesa and Landale (1997). Most of the subjects were identified and chosen in those areas where their specific ethnic groups are highly concentrated (Cubans on the other side of the Hudson River, Dominicans in Washington Heights, and Puerto Ricans in El Barrio). The other subjects were identified and chosen in other areas of the Boroughs of Manhattan and the Bronx. As will be explained in chapter three, the selection of subjects was carefully controlled for variables such as age and gender.

The second phase of the data collection process involved the administration of a questionnaire. The main purpose of the questionnaire was to gather sociolinguistic information that would help create a profile of the individual, and more importantly, of the particular generations and ethnic groups. This information is summarized and discussed in detail in chapter four.

Finally, phase three of the data collection process consisted of an informal interview. All the subjects who completed a questionnaire were also interviewed. These interviews lasted an average of 38.4 minutes. Three minutes of each interview were selected at random and orthographically transcribed; then the investigator identified the contexts where the selected phonemes may and should undergo the phonetic phenomena to be studied, and made a phonetic transcription (see chapters three and five for more details). The results of this analysis are presented in chapter five. This chapter also includes the results of a statistical analysis that correlates the findings in chapter four with the phonetic transcription. Chapter six presents the conclusions of the study.

COMMUNITIES AND NETWORKS

The identification and selection of subjects for the study involved making decisions that merit explanation. These decisions are related to the construct of *speech community*. Many linguists have hypothesized about the existence of an 'ideal' speech community and their ideas cover—or exclude—a wide spectrum of notions. Bloomfield (1933, 42), for instance, simply characterizes such communities as "a group of people who interact by means of speech." Gumperz goes further and describes such a community as "a social group which may be either monolingual or multilingual, held together by frequency of social interaction patterns and set off from the surrounding areas by weaknesses in the lines of communication " (1971, 101). This de-emphasis of a single language or single variety led him to propose the term *linguistic community* instead. Thus, according to Gumperz, the relationship between communities, as well as the individual's sense of community, play an important role in determining membership and participation. The key element is that the members "show linguistic peculiarities that warrant special study" (114). Labov's definition also shifts the emphasis away from the use of a common language and focuses on rules shared by the speakers. He argues that "these norms may be observed in overt types of evaluative behavior, and by the uniformity of abstract patterns of variation which are invariant in respect to particular levels of usage" (1972, 120–21). Finally, researchers like Milroy (1987) prefer the concept of *network*. In this definition, individuals may have a multiplex network with another if they are tied in a variety of ways (i.e., more than one type of relationship), or if they are related in a single way, the network is said to be a uniplex network.

A problem arises if we try to circumscribe to a specific definition. In the present study, for example, friendships and family ties related many of the subjects to other subjects. However, the nature of the study (questionnaire and interview) and the need to control variables made the utilization of subjects from one single area (block, neighborhood, etc.) impossible. The database consists, rather, of data from more than one speech/linguistic community or network, more than one community (for each generation of each ethnic group) within the New York City metropolitan area. Therefore, the common-ground elements that the subjects have are the immigration experience, common language, and common origin for the first-generation members of the same ethnic background. Second-generation members of the same ethnic background, on the other hand, share a common origin of ascendants and a common linguistic environment: the New York City area. Ethnicity provides a tight connection among individuals, intraethnic interactions are strong, and they have a clear sense of community. Moreover, their linguistic idiosyncrasies do warrant special study and can be described in a coherent manner.

SUMMARY

Essentially, we will present a sociolinguistic profile of the first- and second-generation speakers of Spanish with roots in Cuba, the Dominican Republic, and Puerto Rico and living in the greater New York City metropolitan area, and will compare the phonetic realization of specific phonemes in first- and second-generation speakers of these dialects. These issues are part of a broader question concerning the status of the Spanish language in the United States.

Chapter Two
Spanish in the United States

Most linguistic phenomena, like most studied phenomena, can be explained alluding to forces of various origins. The status of Spanish in the United States is not an exception. The successes in language maintenance, as well as total linguistic loss and assimilation, have their roots in clearly established and well-documented facts. These facts may be of a political, historical, and/or sociolinguistic nature. Languages have always been an integral component of political agendas, for they are associated with unity, similarities among people, and even power. This connection between language and politics has generated many historical events and contexts, which in turn have created unique sociolinguistic environments, like those in which Hispanics/ Latinos function in this country.

This chapter presents a theoretical framework that serves as a point of departure for this study. The first section explores some of the political and historical events that have affected and still affect Hispanics/Latinos and their mother tongue today. The second section summarizes the main aspects presented in the literature on Spanish in the United States. Special attention is given to sociolinguistic factors and domains of language usage. The second generation is the focus of section three, while sections four and five focus on the ethnic groups included in this study.

TWO SELVES AND TWO LANGUAGES

From its very beginnings, the population of this nation has grown primarily as a result of immigration. For years, Europeans sought fortune and a better life in the young United States of America. Many came to this country with a language different from that brought by the "fathers" and "founders," and with a lifestyle that clashed with that being gestated as "American." The result has been duality: two selves and two languages. Newcomers had to learn new ways of doing even the simplest things, and new ways to express ideas, ideas that many times were necessary for surviving.

Let us consider the duality of the self, without leaving the linguistic aspect of this issue entirely aside. In most cases, the image of the self is experienced, expressed, and validated through the individual's ethnicity and ethnic association, and through culture (which many agree includes language). All these elements seem to be questioned and analyzed once an individual becomes an immigrant, and the process may cross generational lines regardless of acculturation in the new land.

The generational factor helps put it in perspective and explain the results of this questioning and analyzing. Different generations deal with ethnicity in different ways, as Fishman (1966a) points out. For instance, he claims that Church, other organizations, and familial remnants of traditional ethnicity help the second generation retain attachment to their ethnicity, and that this generation does not feel like a fragmented part of society in general, as the first generation typically does. Furthermore, since this is not enough for language maintenance, members of the second generation simply maintain a positive attitude towards the ethnic language and culture, an attitude that becomes more evident through adulthood (395–396). In the third generation, the elements mentioned above suffer even more drastically. Fishman argues that these individuals are more selective when it comes to ethnicity; many times they end up viewing the mother tongue as "a cultural or instrumental desideratum and viewing ethnicity as an area of appreciation or a field of study" (396). The author goes on to say:

> While language maintenance becomes a progressively weaker and smaller component of such ethnicity, organizational (including religious) involvement, cultural interests, and modified-disjointed festive acts become relatively more prominent and are maintained much longer. Thus it is that the most striking fact of all comes into focus–that a vast amount of marginal ethnicity can exist side by side with the gradual disappearance of language maintenance, with the two phenomena interacting and contributing to each other. (396)

These words represent encouragement in terms of the retention of some of the aspects that constitute the self in the form of ethnicity and culture. Fishman considers these "stable phenomena." Language, on the other hand, seems to be adversely affected by the prolonged contact with mainstream society, more so than ethnic and cultural identity. The author emphasizes that maintenance of mother tongue in this country is higher "among those immigrants who have maintained greatest psychological, social, and cultural distance from the institutions, processes, and values of

American core society" (396). This statement suggests, thus, that "foreign" languages in the United States have a better chance of surviving if their speakers are able to maintain their culture and ways of being intact, unaltered by their new environment. In other words, and according to this view, marginalization fosters language maintenance.

The situation described above points to the importance of the constitution of a given ethnic group in linguistic phenomena; those factors that make a group behave as an active and unique collectivity in intergroup contexts must be considered. Several researchers have referred to this as *ethnolinguistic vitality* (Giles, Bourhis, and Taylor 1977, cited in Hamers and Blanc 1989, 162). Briefly, the vitality of a group is evaluated based on objective factors, namely status, demography, and institutional support. This framework allows one to classify a group's (objective and perceived) vitality as high, medium, or low. "It is argued that the higher the vitality the more likely a group and its language(s) are to survive as a distinctive entity" (Hamers and Blanc, 163). Therefore, it is suggested that a group's social characterization may be a strong indicator of how its language will deal with the pressure of being a minority language.

Giles and Byrne (1982, cited in Hamers and Blanc 1989) present a model that is intimately related to the concept mentioned above. According to this model, certain factors allow minority group members to become balanced bilinguals. Those factors are (a) a weak identity with their own cultural group and the idea that cultural identity is not dependent on language; (b) the perception that there are no alternatives to the inferior social status of the cultural group; (c) low perception of the vitality of their own group; (d) perception that social group mobility is easy; and (e) stronger identification with categories other than language and culture, such as profession. On the other hand, non-native competence in L2 (English in the United States) develops if these dimensions have opposite values. Hamers and Blanc question the effectiveness of this model due to its emphasis on psychological factors.

Let us focus on language in more depth. Fishman (1966b) discusses and criticizes what has been the policy of the United States government and the establishment. In particular, he denounces the tendency to annihilate the language duality for uniformity's sake. This, as he sees it, has detrimental repercussions in society. As he puts it, "our political and cultural foundations are weakened when large population groupings do not feel encouraged to express, to safeguard, and to develop behavioral patterns that are traditionally meaningful to them" (374–375). Language plays an important role in this statement, for what is meaningful to a particular group is many times expressed via language. This statement is still valid almost forty years later.

The author also points out a situation that is equally valid in today's society: the irony of simultaneously fostering language annihilation and acquisition. He says that

> It is obvious that our national resources of native non-English language competence are allowed–even encouraged–to languish and disappear at the very time that unprecedented efforts and sums are being spent to improve and increase the teaching of "foreign" languages in the nation's schools and colleges. (371)

This persists today, as language courses are added to curricula and degree requirements because of the advantage an individual has when he or she is competent in a language other than English. Nevertheless, are immigrants encouraged to freely use those languages being taught in schools and colleges?

According to Fishman, one of the ways in which the government has controlled for duality is restriction of immigration (379). In this article from 1966 he argues that the United States is admitting fewer immigrants and that those admitted into the country are less likely to "perpetuate their non-English mother tongues" (379). The author characterizes this group of ideal immigrants as educated and skilled (primarily for technological employment), and as he claims, "These characteristics have various implications for language maintenance" (379). In Fishman's view, the more an individual can offer to the country based on their education and preparation, the less of a threat they will pose to the linguistic and cultural stability of the country. The assumption behind this idea is that when individuals join the labor force of the new country, they automatically become candidates for assimilation by the dominant group, and this assimilation includes language.

Fishman presents some ideological solutions and recommendations. First, he claims that

> language maintenance efforts are justifiable and desirable because: either they serve the *national* interest (both in utilitarian and in an idealistic sense), and/or they promote various *group* interests that need not be in conflict with the national interest, and/or they contribute powerfully to the enrichment of *individual* functioning. (374)

This, as he mentions, allows people to benefit from each language, maturely and freely, rather than from one language or the other. Going against this precept would be inexplicable, given the almost universal human right to communicate, regardless of the choice of code. He adds that "every nation, new or old, that engages in language maintenance efforts must define the domains (if any) in which cultural and linguistic unity must receive precedence over cultural and linguistic diversity" (373).

In sum, the immigration experience forces people to evaluate their own identity, and if the motherland and the new land do not share the same linguistic code, to make conscious and unconscious linguistic decisions. Identity aspects appear to prevail. Some of its components, perhaps the most representative are transmitted from generation to generation, and descendants of immigrants, succeed in maintaining some level of connection with those elements that characterize their ancestors' ethnicity and culture. Language, on the other hand, falls in a different category. It is more vulnerable to change, partly because of the impact that immigration and political policies, and continuous contact with the new culture of the new setting have on the linguistic behavior of immigrants. As Portes and Schauffler explain (1994, 643),

> In the past, the typical pattern has been for the first generation to learn enough English to survive economically; the second generation continued to speak the parental tongue at home, but English in school, at work and in public life; by the third generation, the home language shifted to English, which effectively became the mother tongue for subsequent generations.

We have already described what can be considered the fate of immigrant languages in the United States. In the next section, we review the literature on the Spanish language in this country.

THE CASE OF THE SPANISH LANGUAGE AND THE SPANISH SPEAKERS IN THE UNITED STATES

Before beginning to understand the status of Spanish in the United States, it is imperative to consider some demographic data. In this country, the four major Hispanic/Latino groups are the Mexican-origin population (58.8 percent of the total), the Puerto Rican population (9.6 percent of the total), the Cuban-origin population (3.5 percent of the total), and the 'Other-Spanish'-origin population (28.4 percent of the total) (U.S. Bureau of the Census 2001, 2). This last group includes people from Spain and other Spanish-speaking countries in Central and South America. The first three groups have had distinctive geographical patterns of settlement. Mexicans have occupied the southwestern part of the United States (from California to Texas). Puerto Ricans and Cubans, on the other hand, have settled in large urban areas in New York and Florida, respectively (Y. R. Solé 1990, 35–36).

Historically, Hispanics/Latinos have had to face and deal with a linguistic controversy upon arrival: living in a society in which the dominant language is not Spanish. This dichotomy has had and continues to have

interesting repercussions for descendants of Hispanics/Latinos and other individuals who come to the United States at an early age. Generally speaking,
the retention rates of Spanish are high. There has been an uninterrupted
transmission of Spanish from generation to generation across decades.
"Hispanics show a high degree of Spanish maintenance even among the native-born" (Bean and Tienda 1987, 259).

According to Y. R. Solé (1987, 162), in 1980, 77 percent of Hispanics/
Latinos had retained their ancestral language versus only 59 percent of
European descents. Cuban-Americans have the highest retention rate (75.5
percent), followed by Puerto Ricans (66.7 percent), Mexican-Americans
(64.6 percent), and the 'Other-Spanish' sub-group (60.4 percent). Each
group shows more Spanish maintenance in those areas where its members
are the most represented. Thus, Cuban-Americans have higher degrees of
maintenance in Florida, Puerto Ricans in New York, and Mexican-
Americans and Chicanos in the Southwest (Y. R. Solé 1990, 39–40).

In most cases, however, the solution to the aforementioned linguistic
controversy has been a movement toward bilingualism. The acquisition
and use of the Spanish and English linguistic codes remain as "the dominant pattern of accommodation to the American environment" (38).
Bilingualism among Hispanics/Latinos, nevertheless, is restricted by levels
of English and Spanish fluency. In 1980, approximately half of the adult
population had good English skills, one fourth had fair skills, and the
other fourth had problems with these skills. That is, three out of every four
Hispanics/Latinos had "good" to "very good" English competence. Puerto
Ricans claimed to have "good" to "very good" English competence more
often (80 percent), followed by the 'Other Spanish' subgroup (73.5 percent). Seventy percent of Mexican-Americans and Cuban-Americans made
this claim. As implied before, these levels of bilingualism per group decrease in those areas where each group is the most concentrated
Hispanic/Latino group, though generally speaking, Colorado, New
Mexico, and Arizona had the highest percentages of English dominant individuals and the lowest percentages of individuals with deficient English
skills. Texas, New York, California, and Florida had the highest percentages of Spanish monolinguals and of incipient bilinguals (Y. R. Solé 1987,
166). Finally, and including children under the age of 5 who do not speak
English either, the number of Hispanics/Latinos who spoke only Spanish
was almost 2.5 million (163).

The linguistic situation of Hispanics/Latinos in the United States is
intimately related to the environment. Historically, certain ethnic groups
have settled in urban areas and others have settled in rural areas. Scholars

have tried to take this issue into consideration in order to determine how the socioeconomic context affects language. Y. R. Solé (1990), for instance, argues that large cities are more prone to foster retention than less expanded settings. She claims that the presence of minority groups in large cities facilitates their segregation into areas with a distinctive social identity, which, in turn, fosters isolation and marginalization from the dominant group. The presence of a sizable number of immigrants, on the other hand, retards the linguistic assimilation of the group as a whole, as numerous recent immigrants require that the members of the minority group retain some proficiency in the minority language to communicate with them (57). Hudson-Edwards and Bills (1980) dispute this claim. As their study in Martineztown, New Mexico, shows Spanish retention is facilitated in smaller areas. Sánchez (1982) says that this is due to the precarious economic situation of Chicanos and Mexican-Americans in the Southwest. She claims that

> low-income jobs lead to the concentration of the minority population in ghettos and barrios, where housing is cheap and where one can rely on friends and relatives for assistance during moments of crisis [. . .]. The concentration of the Spanish-speaking population in certain residential areas is thus a result of poverty and racial discrimination and is largely responsible for the maintenance of Spanish. (10)

Regardless of whether Hispanics/Latinos in the United States and their descendants fit the criteria to be considered Spanish or English monolinguals or bilinguals, most of them have a high regard for Spanish. In 1966, Hayden found that this regard for Spanish varied among groups. More Hispanics/Latinos in New York City (72 percent) than Hispanics/Latinos in San Antonio (57 percent) thought that the preservation of Spanish was necessary. However, more people in San Antonio (43 percent) were actively involved in its preservation than in New York City (35 percent) (195). Despite this low level of involvement, quite a few families in these communities assisted their children in learning the mother tongue (197).

A study conducted in two New York City communities by García et al. (1988) showed that Hispanics/Latinos wanted their children to be bilingual and biliterate, i.e., they wanted their children to have native-like English and Spanish competence. This attitude toward Spanish is based on parents' desire for their children to be able to communicate with other native speakers of Spanish and with relatives from their countries of origin. They support the use of Spanish as a private and public means of communication, with the ulterior motive of maintaining Spanish as an instrument for the maintenance of culture. These individuals, however, claim to use both Spanish and English to address their parents, siblings, and children (more common among Puerto Ricans and Cubans than among Dominicans and Colombians).

Hidalgo's (1993) study of Mexican-Americans from Chula Vista, California, presents results that include both parents' and the children's opinions, and a very different scenario as well. These results indicate that parents see more value in Spanish, especially when it comes to doing business in their community and when traveling in Spanish-speaking countries. The younger generation feels less strongly about Spanish because of the role of English for personal and developmental purposes. Parents use more Spanish than their children at home, in the neighborhood, in the community, in personal communications, and in the mass media. English permeates public interaction among the younger generation. The author attributes these findings to different levels of bilingualism.

If Hispanics/Latinos in the United States want the Spanish language to survive, why is there a trend toward bilingualism and consequent English monolingualism? What are the forces that play a part in Hispanics/Latinos' linguistic choices? The answer to these questions may lie in the social aspects that surround Hispanics/Latinos in this country and in the role of Spanish as a subordinate language. There are several issues to consider. First, transmission of a minority language from generation to generation requires certain kind of support from the community, and perhaps more important, from society in general. Generally, "it is usually very difficult for children to acquire active command of a minority language, where that language does not receive [this kind of] support" (Romaine 1995, 186). Secondly, as C. A. Solé puts it (1980, 277), "Once an individual acquires a second language and this one happens to be the dominant language of his geographic habitat, he is then faced with the problem of choosing or alternating between the two." Moreover, Hispanics/Latinos in the United States have had a history of low social status among Americans, and this status, in turn, has given Spanish a poor reputation. Consequently, and as in many other cases where a dominant language and a minority language coexist,

> the dominant language is associated with status, prestige and social success. It is used in the 'glamour' contexts in the wider society—for formal speeches on ceremonial occasions, by news readers on television and radio, and by those whom young people admire—pop stars, fashion models, and disc jockeys. It is scarcely surprising that many young minority group speakers should see its advantages and abandon their own language. (Holmes 1994, 61)

Y. R. Solé (1980, 287) sheds more light on this matter. In an attempt to illustrate the language choice process of Hispanics/Latinos (and of any other group in the same sociolinguistic context), she suggests that the outcome is the result of the interplay of several factors: personal need of the individual versus group demand, the need to preserve intragroup identification versus the desire to identify with the outgroup, and the congruence or incongruence between the demands made by the ingroup versus the outgroup. Thus, in her opinion, the social environment determines what position an individual takes with regard to language; this position is based on an individual's needs in this environment, the role that conservation or loss of the ancestral tongue plays in group membership, and the inner constitution and needs of the group of speakers of the ancestral tongue.

SOCIOLINGUISTIC FACTORS AND THE RETENTION AND USE OF SPANISH

Many works have centered on the role of specific sociolinguistic aspects on the continuum between Spanish language maintenance and English monolingualism. These factors have proved to be immensely revealing and important because they help us understand the conditions governing placement and even shifts in this continuum. As Silva-Corvalán says (1994, 220–21), speaking about bilingualism in Los Angeles,

> Hispanic communities [. . .] give evidence of the wondrously complex sociolinguistic phenomenon of societal bilingualism: Spanish illustrates a continuum of levels of proficiency along which speakers move, up or down, either in their lifetime or across generations (there is also a clear proficiency continuum in English). This is a dynamic situation which, given enough time and favorable conditions, may lead to a cycle of changes.

The following is a summary of some of those conditions that Silva-Corvalán alludes to:

Gender. Women claim Spanish as their dominant language somewhat more than men. This suggests that women, through their maternal role, have more influence than men in determining language issues. Women, on the other hand, also claim to be less English dominant than men. To be precise, one out of every four women versus one out of every five men are Spanish dominant (Y. R. Solé 1990). Portes and Schauffler (1994) also argue that women retain their parental language more often than men and speculate that this is attributable to the seclusion of female youth in the home environment, which exposes them to greater contact with parents. Zentella (1982) supports these findings in the Puerto Rican community in New York City under the same assumption. Hidalgo (1993) arrives at the same conclusions with data from Chula Vista, California. The author suggests that this has to do with the fact that success is expected more from boys than from girls (66). Klee (1987) makes the opposite claim. She reports a greater shift to English by Mexican-American females than by males because they are "more likely to accept outgroup values" (131).

Economic Status. López (1982) demonstrated that Spanish maintenance is associated with low economic status, measured by years of schooling, occupational prestige, and income. There seems to be, however, a different direct association between Spanish maintenance, high educational attainment, and English competence. This is an important factor because, as García (1995) says, the establishment wants to blame Hispanics/Latinos' economic failure on Spanish, even when the economy in general has shrunk. Similarly, Portes and Schauffler (1994) point out that since wealthier and educated parents can provide the opportunities for their children to enter the mainstream culture and acquire English, their intentions of promoting parental language retention are unfruitful. Other authors have established a relationship between income and language maintenance (Veltman 1983; Fishman 1984; Hart-González 1990), but they point out that the relationship is not one of cause and effect. There are two reasons for this conclusion. First, African Americans and most Latinos have not attained an enormous economic success despite their high rates of assimilation. Second, Cuban-Americans have attained significant economic success despite their low levels of assimilation. As Bean and Tienda (1987) say to explain why Cubans are more economically successful despite being less proficient in English than Mexicans and Puerto Ricans, "while mastery of English may be a necessary condition for socioeconomic success, it is insufficient by itself" (94).

Education. The most educated Hispanics/Latinos tend to be less Spanish-retentive than those less educated in California, New York, Illinois, and Texas. Hayden (1966, 363), however, claims the opposite by saying that "the presence of substantial intellectual or professional class, or of a large middle class, strengthened the institution that supported language use directly." The author points out that, paradoxically, Mexican-Americans in the Southwest show less Spanish attrition than any other group.

Occupational Categories. There is some evidence that higher occupational categories are linked to less Spanish retention. This might be explained as occupational upward mobility at the expense of Spanish retention (Y. R. Solé 1990). C. A. Solé (1980) says that fathers with a high level of educational achievement influence more English use among their children. Research findings, however, are mixed. Portes and Schauffler (1994) claim that the occupational factor is irrelevant because it does not really point to any significant differences in Spanish retention among individuals.

Age. The youngest and the oldest individuals—children under five and adults over 60—tend to be either incipient bilinguals or Spanish monolinguals. Among pre-school children this tendency is stronger when parents and grandparents are foreign born. Among older Hispanics/Latinos, Spanish monolingualism increases in those places with large numbers of foreign-born-Hispanics/Latinos (Y. R. Solé 1990). In addition, in a study in Martineztown, an Albuquerque barrio, Hudson-Edwards and Bills (1980) found that most of the subjects over 25 years of age claim at least good fluency in Spanish and that those 25 or under were fairly evenly distributed on a three point ability scale. Of the first group, 75 percent use Spanish as the main home language, whereas 25 percent use Spanish to the total exclusion of English. In terms of age, C. A. Solé (1980) says that what is really relevant in the case of foreign-born individuals is age of arrival in the United States. In another study, conducted in the Rio Grande Valley by Klee (1987), 94 percent of adults reported having learned Spanish as their first language while only 54 percent of the student population made the same claim. Nine percent of the teenagers learned both languages simultaneously and 37 percent learned English first. In terms of proficiency, 17 percent of the adults claimed to be more proficient in English while 44 percent of the teenagers made this claim. Finally, only 16 percent of the teenagers feel more proficient in Spanish compared to 42 percent of the adults (128). Age is also an important issue because, as Stone states (1987, 152), individuals' most active use of the Spanish language is with older adults. Spanish-language loss may accelerate rapidly in the future, when there will be fewer adults with whom to speak.

Mother Tongue. Communicative ability in Spanish correlates strongly with claims of Spanish as the mother tongue in Martineztown, New Mexico. Eighty percent of those who claimed Spanish as their mother tongue reported to be fluent in Spanish, whereas the majority of those who claimed English also claimed to be weak in Spanish. Among the bilingual mother tongue claimants, only 20 percent are fluent in Spanish while 90 percent are fluent in English. Fewer than half of the subjects reported using Spanish as the primary home language, 19 percent use Spanish and English, and over one third prefer English over Spanish. The junior generation, nevertheless, has fewer chances than the senior generation to develop native-like competence in Spanish despite having been exposed to Spanish as their mother tongue (Hudson-Edwards and Bills 1980, 145).

Family Structure. C. A. Solé (1980) argues that an extended family structure undoubtedly contributes to language retention, although no solid arguments are presented to support this claim.

Context of Interaction. Otheguy and García (1993) claim that when speakers interact with an interlocutor and deal with the same topics in a North American context and in a Latin American context, low levels of English-based hibridization are produced in the Latin American context vis-à-vis the North American context (149). They attribute these findings to the idea that different contexts call for different conceptualizations (150).

Closeness to the Homeland. Glazer (1966) points out that mother tongues are maintained longer where immigrant groups are almost geographic extensions of homelands than where immigrants are geographically cut-off from their homelands. The author gives the examples of French Canadians in New England, Puerto Ricans in New York, Cubans in Florida, and Mexicans in the Southwest. Relative concentration of immigrants' settlements also plays an important role (362).

It is important to point out that retention of Spanish in the Southwest cannot be explained as the mere interplay of economic, educational, and occupational factors. On the contrary, economic progress has increased Spanish retention and closer ties with Mexico in the Southwest (Grebler, Moore, and Guzmán 1970, cited in Y. R. Solé 1990). In this region, demographic concentrations of Mexican-Americans, segregation, and strong ethnic and cultural ties have influenced Spanish retention among this population (Sánchez 1982; Y. R. Solé 1990). Moreover, C. A. Solé (1980) states that these issues have been more influential than ideological conviction or elaboration on behalf of Spanish. Many of these findings can be explained in terms of domains of linguistic usage, which is the focus of the next section.

DOMAINS

In a language contact situation, maintenance and its interplay with sociolinguistic, ethnic, and cultural factors cannot be explained without taking domains of language use into consideration. Context of use plays an important part in defining language relevance, especially when two or more languages are competing for predominance and/or survival. The literature has captured this aspect of language. Fishman (1971) provides an excellent definition and rationale:

> Domains are defined, regardless of their number, in terms of institutional context and their congruent behavioral co-occurrence. They attempt to summate the major clusters of interaction that occur in clusters of multilingual settings and involving clusters of interlocutors. Domains enable us to understand that language choice and topic, appropriate though may be for analyses of individual behavior at the level of face-to-face verbal encounters, are [. . .] related to widespread social/cultural

norms and expectations. By recognizing the existence of domains it becomes possible to contrast the language of topics for individuals or particular sub-populations with the predominant language of domains for larger networks, if not the whole, of a speech community. (586)

As Fishman states, society and culture develop and impose certain norms that govern topics of conversation, and these norms manifest themselves at the one-on-one level of interaction as well as at a broader level of interaction (network/speech community). These norms determine the linguistic tools that the interlocutor brings to the interaction to create or maintain an effect of an affective nature.

In a study about domains, Hayden (1966) compares data representative of the Mexican-American, Puerto Rican, Ukrainian, and French communities in the United States. The report claims that the relative success that Hispanics/Latinos have had at retaining their mother tongue may be attributed to its use in the home domain. This is "primarily responsible for enabling children to attain mastery of it" (198). Apparently, this has the effect of making individuals prefer the mother tongue on more occasions than is comfortable or practical, such as with children, siblings, acquaintances, at work, or while shopping (201). Hayden claims that discrimination and hostility, however, make some speakers from the Puerto Rican community (those more "practical" and "sensitive") suppress the use of Spanish in these contexts. There is evidence of the same in the San Antonio community, despite the fact that one third to one half of the population is of Hispanic/Latino extraction (202).

The generational issue also enters in interplay with domains. In a study conducted in a community in the Rio Grande Valley, Klee (1987) reports that generational differences of interlocutors determine language usage in the home environment. In other contexts, such as work and church, the domain in which the interaction takes place is what determines usage. "In the younger group, interlocutor of the same age, whether they be friends, cousins, siblings, classmates, or neighbors, tend to be addressed in the same way in terms of language choice regardless of domain" (129).

Linguistic competence is another aspect of language that seems to be affected by domains. For example, Silva-Corvalán (1992) establishes a correlation between level of linguistic competence and use domains for a given language. After analyzing data from bilingual children in Los Angeles she concludes that those who communicate relatively less frequently in Spanish show a relatively low level of competence in Spanish. Thus, for children, the more domains in which they use Spanish, the more competent they will be in the language. Silva-Corvalán uses this argument to dismantle the notion that

Spanish acquisition impedes English acquisition in bilingual children. She implies that, when children are exposed to both languages in different domains, both languages will have the opportunity to develop, and English will reach competence levels equal to those of the monolingual children (237–238).

Several studies have focused on specific ethnic groups and communities, and revealed information about how domains operate in them. Let us consider the Puerto Rican community of New York City. Hoffman (1971) ties the Spanish maintenance in this community to family, kinship, and ethnicity (23). The author says:

> The more one functions within [the domain encompassed by] the Puerto Rican value system, the more he would be compelled to speak the language or language variant required by that system. As a person moves farther away from an exclusively Puerto Rican value orientation his freedom of language choice increases, subject only to the constraints imposed by new value orientations. (25)

Thus, the value system changes outside of the neighborhood, while linguistic freedom takes over. However, the barrio remains "primarily a Spanish situational context" (28). It is relevant to mention another point that Hoffman makes: Parents who are not completely proficient in English learn enough English vocabulary to let their children know that they can function within their new domain, and that they are familiar with the associated values of this domain (38). This exposes adults to a value system different from the one in the community and fosters their acquisition of English, although limited.

Greefield and Fishman (1971) also touch on the relationship between values, Spanish, and domains within the Puerto Rican community. They argue that in this group, intimacy and solidarity are associated with Spanish in domains such as family and friendship. English, on the other hand, is associated with status differentiation and domains such as religion, education, employment, and the like. These languages are clearly polarized (235). They allude to a diglossic situation governed by the aforementioned three-part relationship (243). According to C. A. Solé, (1982, 259), this is not the case among Cuban-Americans. In his opinion, language choice among members of this group does not respond to diglossia. He points out linguistic competence of the speakers as the determining factor, which in turn is determined by generational differences, years of residence, and age at time of arrival.

THE CURRENT SITUATION

As we can see, a discussion about the status of the Spanish language in the United States has to be intimately linked to different levels of English proficiency, populations, sociolinguistic issues, and geography. Although it is too premature to arrive at a consensus that would allow us to foresee the fate of Spanish in this country, data hint at the fact that loss to English will continue among many Hispanics/Latinos in many communities. Evidently, the tendency is toward incipient bilingualism and certain ciphers raise concern. Furthermore, the community base is weakening. The minority language is being threatened by the fact that English is becoming the dominant language of this generation and it is likely to become the mother tongue of the next generation.

What can we expect? The literature shows that some scholars are not too optimistic (Gans 1992; Hart-González and Feingold 1990; Hudson-Edwards and Bills 1980; Wald 1987). The issue of language choice and consequent language maintenance or shift may be, as C. A. Solé states (1980, 280), "determined by the linguistic competence of the speakers, which in turn is governed by generational differences, years of residence in the United States, and age at arrival." Floyd (1985) agrees on the need to look closely at age and generational factors as indicators of linguistic behavior.

Let us concentrate on the generational factor, specifically on the internal constitution of the second generation.

THE SECOND GENERATION

The proliferation in the number of second-generation individuals in the United States is a direct consequence of the 1965 amendments to the Immigration and Nationality Act, and the changes in American asylum and refugee policies. As a result, the origin of immigrants shifted from Europe to the Third World. "The percent arriving from Asian and Latin American countries increased from about 30 percent during the 1950s, to about 85 percent today" (Jensen and Chitose 1994, 714). This is what is called the *new immigration.*

An important issue when dealing with the concept of *second generation* is to understand that there are several conceptualizations of the term *generation.* Social scientists have tried to come up with clear-cut definitions, but the lack of agreement among them has impeded the operationalization of one single approach. As Oropesa and Landale say (1997, 431),

> some demographers refer to a generation as "one stage in the succession of natural descent" that is occupied by "all persons of the same genealogical rank" (Petersen and Petersen 1986:356). Other scholars use this term more broadly (or less precisely) and combine elements of more restrictive definitions. This is evident in the descriptions of generations as cohorts or age groups who share "common locations in the social and

historical process" which limit them "to a specific range of potential experience, predisposing them for a certain characteristic mode of thought
and experience." (Mannheim 1952: 291).

This discrepancy translates into a lack of consensus with regard to
what *second generation* entails. In particular, the issues of intermarriage,
family migration, and age upon arrival to the United States play a part in
the notion of *second generation*. For instance, the "new second generation"
refers to the descendants of the most recent wave of immigrants from Asia
and Latin America, whereas the "de facto second generation" includes children who came to the United States at an early age and were exposed to the
American ways in their formative years. Moreover, Oropesa and Landale
mention Rumbaut's (1997) three-part definition that distinguishes between
the "1.25" generation (individuals who arrived as teenagers), the "1.5"
generation (individuals who arrived as pre-teens), and the "1.75" generation (those who arrived as pre-schoolers). With regard to intermarriage,
some consider having one foreign-born parent as the requirement, while
others emphasize the nativity status of the mother, more common in culture
transmission studies.

After analyzing data from the 1990 Census, Oropesa and Landale suggest that, despite these differences, (a) inferences about the composition of the
second generation are not very sensitive to operational criteria, and (b) exceptions which indicate slight sensitivity are due more to decisions about how to
handle the nativity status of the child than the nativity status of the parents.
They argue, however, that native-born children should not be combined with
foreign-born children whenever language is one of the aspects being studied.
The latter group is less likely than the former to be bilingual or English monolingual (odds that increase for the 1.5 and 1.25 generations). Nevertheless,
their findings show that the majority of children are either bilingual or English
monolingual. The chances of being bilingual are higher among Cuban,
Dominican, and Colombian children than Mexican children. The findings of
this study are very important for the research we are discussing here. The key
criterion for classification within the first or second generation was place of
birth, due to the linguistic nature of this investigation.

Several studies have focused specifically on second-generation members
and provide information about their linguistic status. One example is Jensen
and Chitose's study of individuals 25 years or younger (1994). They argue
that in 1990 about 95 percent of children of immigrants were living in metropolitan areas in New York, New Jersey, Connecticut, and Illinois (717).
This number increases if we consider foreign-born individuals who migrated
early in life to be part of the second generation. They add that the typical

second-generation household is slightly larger and has more related children present than the typical first-generation household. These households have fewer rooms and more total persons per bedroom. The official poverty rate is 17 percent and 8.4 percent of second-generation children live in deep poverty. Other facts about second-generation children such as mean age, percent not in school, and sex ratio are virtually the same between native and second-generation children. There are some very positive aspects as well:

> Compared to native children, their household heads are more likely to be married, are overrepresented among the best educated, and have higher self-employment and asset income . . . [In addition,] household heads of second-generation children are less likely to receive welfare income and more likely to receive earnings than are their native counterparts. Finally, the second generation themselves are just as likely to be attending school. (733)

From a linguistic point of view, the modal foreign language spoken in second-generation households is Spanish, followed by Asian-Pacific Island languages. It is important to state that, according to the 1992 report of the U.S. Bureau of the Census (cited in Jensen and Chitose 1994), second-generation children of more recent immigrants are more likely to live in linguistically isolated households, that is, a household in which no one over the age of 14 speaks English at least "very well." Jensen and Chitose also say that about 66 percent of second-generation children are more likely to speak a language other than English at home. Moreover, about 45 percent of second-generation children have a Hispanic/Latino household head, of which only about 24 percent speak English "not well" or "not at all." These heads, interestingly, are equally overrepresented among the poorly and well educated, but the majority has lower earnings and lower occupational status than the native-born. "This reflects an immigration policy that continues to give priority to prospective immigrants with exceptional scientific, professional or artistic credentials" (726). The authors claim that the socioeconomic situation of foreign-born children of immigrants is not as favorable.

Portes and Schauffler's study is another source of information related to members of the second generation (1994). In their study with eighth- and ninth-grade students from different countries in the Caribbean, Central, and South America living in Miami and Ft. Lauderdale, they showed that (a) length of U.S. residence among the second generation has the strongest association with language assimilation; (b) parental status leads toward greater English proficiency but not toward greater bilingualism; and (c) bilingualism varies directly with demographic concentration and economic diversification of the immigrant community and inversely with length of

U.S. residence. Eighty percent of these youngsters preferred English. This preference exists regardless of the type of environment they grew up in, namely, English-only or one in which Spanish is widespread. Latin American nationalities, however, show more probability of retaining their parental language. The authors suggest that there are two main forces playing a part in bilingualism. They explain that,

> while living in a less ethnic environment reduces the likelihood of retaining a foreign language, it does not by itself reduce the probability of becoming bilingual. It is the character of the immigrant community—its diversity, history, and cohesiveness—that seems to hold the key on whether second-generation children successfully combine two languages. On the other hand, length of residence in the country again decreases the probability of bilingualism. (655–656)

Another study is that of Veltman (1990), in which he makes predictions for the year 2001 based on the mother tongue of mainland born Hispanics/Latinos and specific age groups in 1976. He states that, although this population will increase to 21.07 million, 12.50 million people more than in 1976, only 8.04 million people will be added to the Spanish language group. The rest (4.46 million) will have been anglicized. Furthermore, approximately 45 percent of those who frequently speak Spanish may be expected to prefer using English and approximately 18.5 percent will not speak English on a regular basis. Nearly all of them will be elders or recent immigrants. It is important to emphasize, as the author claims, that the main factors that will guarantee a continuous growth in the Hispanic/Latino population of the United States are continued immigration and the fertility level of this group.

In sum, the picture of Spanish language maintenance among second-generation individuals is uncertain and somewhat contradictory. On one hand, we can expect a continuous flow of immigrants that may be enough to compensate for losses to English language shift. On the other hand, history may repeat itself.

We have yet to see if Hispanics/Latinos in the United States are going to triumph over or succumb to the United States unwritten policy of imposing English as a symbol of national unity and nationhood. They may be winning the battle. The language shift trend has been pointed out by Fishman (1964), Floyd (1985), and Holmes (1994), to name a few, and unfortunately, that may mean that we already have the answers to our questions: Hispanics/Latinos have been more successful at maintaining their mother tongue than any other group but levels of proficiency and attitudes, among other issues, raise concerns.

CUBANS, DOMINICANS, AND PUERTO RICANS IN THE MAINLAND: WHO AND HOW THEY ARE

The purpose of this section is to provide a historical, socioeconomic, and linguistic framework of each ethnic group in which to contextualize the study. The information on each group is presented separately.

Cubans

The main factor that influenced the emigration of Cubans to the United States was the rise to power of Fidel Castro. Soon after this historical event in 1959, the middle and upper class came to the United States, escaping from Castro's policy of redistributing wealth. Most of these Cubans were well-educated and arrived with work skills. These Cubans settled in the Miami area. A different group, however, came in the early 1980s, consisting of poorer and socially undesirable people. This group represents those frequently called "Marielitos," whose arrival increased the Cuban population by 27 percent from the 1960s to the 1980s (Gynan 1987, 178). Although most of the "Marielitos" also sought to establish themselves in Miami, many moved North toward New York City. This new influx dramatically altered the composition of the Cuban population in this area, which had consisted mostly of well educated individuals with promising economic futures.

According to data from the 1990 Census, Cubans have a median household income of $27,741; 11.4 percent live in poverty, and 51.1 percent are homeowners. With regard to education, 56.6 percent of Cubans are high school graduates whereas 16.5 percent are college graduates (Grasmuck and Grosfoguel 1997, 341). The unemployment rate among Cubans is 13.3 percent. The main industries of employment are transportation, communications, utilities, wholesale, and retail trades (30.6 percent); manufacturing (19.5 percent); and social services (17.2 percent) (347). More recent data from the 2000 Census show that 3.7 percent of all Hispanics are of Cuban descent (U.S. Bureau of the Census 2003, 1). Furthermore, 70.8 percent of Cubans 25 years or older have at least a high school education (5). Finally, 34.3 percent of them have an annual income of $35,000 or more and 16.5 percent lives below the poverty level (U.S. Bureau of the Census 2001, 6).

Cuban-Americans constitute the greatest Spanish monolingual group in the United States. One percent of Cubans between the ages of 15 and 17, and 33 percent of Cubans 18 years old or over claim that the language usually spoken by them is Spanish (Portes and Rumbaut 1996, 215). It is also the group with the highest percentage of speakers who claim to be fluent in English (98.8 percent) as well as that with the highest percentage of speakers who claim to be fluent in Spanish (94.2 percent) (259). Y. R. Solé (1987, 166) gives somewhat different figures. She argues that 45 percent of the Cuban population is English dominant, 23 percent has good English skills, and almost one third of the population has problems with English or does not have any skills. In addition, the 1990 Census reveals that 5 percent of Cubans 5 years old or over speak only English at home while 95 percent speak only Spanish (Portes and Rumbaut 1996, 208).

García et al. (1988) is one of the few linguistic studies that take into consideration Cuban-Americans in New York City. The author states that almost half of the Cuban parents in New York City claim speaking English or English and Spanish to their children. In the authors' opinion, this situation will give Cuban-American children a very slight chance of becoming fully proficient in Spanish. This prediction is based on the fact that these children rarely spend time in a Spanish monolingual society and that the Cuban society in New York City is not as unified as that in Dade County or in New Jersey.

Cubans are responsible for the status of Spanish in Miami, Florida. According to García (1995), the level of acceptance that Spanish has obtained in Dade County has to do with several factors that have made it less marked. First, its speakers (who are mostly Cuban-Americans) have a higher level of income and education. Second, they are more often considered white than other Latino groups in the United States. This makes Spanish less marked than in other areas of the United States and makes it possible for its speakers to push for equal treatment. Third, the political situation surrounding Cuban-Americans in the United States has been favorable for this group also. The author argues that

> the Anglo majority views these speakers of Spanish with less suspicion than those who still hold political allegiances to their homelands. This makes it possible for the Anglo majority to enter negotiation for equality of treatment of these Spanish speakers. (155)

Fourth, Spanish in Dade County is the language of the most powerful business firms owned by Spanish speakers in the United States, a power from which the majority can also profit. Finally, the large influx of Latinos from other countries and from other places in the United States into Dade County adds to the density of Spanish and to the value of Spanish as an instrument of communication. García adds:

> This has been done by entering into a dynamic cycle in which the language minority pushes for equality of treatment by emphasizing the decreased markedness of Spanish, the majority responds by entering the negotiation accepting the decreased foreignness of Spanish, the minority

engages the majority in negotiation by focusing on the socioeconomic power of Spanish, and finally the minority continues to define Spanish as a resource for intraethnic communication. (155–56)

Bean and Tienda (1987) also point out the relationship between socioeconomical success and the incorporation experience that distinguishes Cubans from other groups. The factors that they identify are (a) that the early immigrants were political rather than economic refugees; (b) the over-representation of highly educated individuals during the early phase of the exodus from Cuba; and (c) acceptance by a federal government eager to provide refuge from a Communist dictatorship (28). Despite these privileged conditions, Bean and Tienda believe that "English will [still] become the dominant language both within and outside the household" (93).

Dominicans

The out-migration of Dominicans to the United States was also motivated by political reasons, in particular, the dictatorship of General Trujillo. In 1961, when the general was assassinated, the United States consulate facilitated the acquisition of visas in order to avoid the development of a political system like that of Cuba. The support of the then governor of the Dominican Republic, Joaquín Balaguer, motivated this exodus, which increased substantially due to the poor economic conditions in the country in the late 70s and 80s. In fact, the Dominican population in the United Sates increased 58 percent in two decades (Gynan 1987, 178). The majority of the newly arriving Dominicans were from the small and middle peasantry of the Cibao region as well as from the urban lower middle class of Santo Domingo and Santiago. Their preferred destination was New York City, specifically, deteriorating neighborhoods in Washington Heights, the Lower East Side, and the Corona section of Queens.

According to the 1990 Census, the percentage of Dominicans that live below the poverty line is 33.4. The median household income, on the other hand, is $20,006; 13.4 percent are homeowners. In terms of education, 42.6 percent are high school graduates and 7.8 percent are college graduates (Grasmuck and Grosfoguel 1997, 341). The unemployment rate among Dominicans is 17.8 percent. The main industries of employment are transportation, communications, utilities, wholesale, and retail trades (34.1 percent); manufacturing (27.4 percent); and social services (14.3 percent) (347). Linguistically speaking, 4 percent of Dominicans 5 years old or over use only English at home whereas 96 percent use only Spanish (Portes and Rumbaut 1996, 209). Finally, and according to the 2000 Census, 2.2 percent of all Hispanics are Dominican (U.S. Bureau of the Census 2001, 2).

The number of sociological and linguistic studies that include specific information about Dominicans in the United States is extremely limited. In fact, most of the studies that consider data from different Hispanic/Latino groups do not consider Dominicans as a separate group. This lack of information is tied to the fact that Dominican Americans became a significant population only during the 1980s. They are now one of the ethnic groups with the highest growth in population in New York City. One study, however, sheds some light on the linguistic profile of Dominicans. It claims that, at home, Dominicans in this city use more Spanish than Cubans and Puerto Ricans, but slightly less than Central and South Americans (García et al. 1988, 496). Overall figures are not provided.

Puerto Ricans

New York City started seeing a substantial in-migration of Puerto Ricans in the latter years of World War II. The deploring economic situation of the island as opposed to the increasingly fruitful economy of the mainland motivated Puerto Ricans to make this move. The growing garment industry demanded high numbers of unskilled workers and this group responded to the recruitment movements. The largest number came during the 50s and settled in declining areas within the city.

The profile of the Puerto Rican community based on the 1990 Census is as follows: 29.6 percent lives below the poverty line, 26 percent own their own homes, 53.4 percent have a high school diploma, and 9.4 percent are college graduates. The median household income is $21,056 (Grasmuck and Grosfoguel 1997, 341). The unemployment rate among Puerto Ricans is 14.1 percent, and the main industries of employment are social services (32.3 percent); transportation, communications, utilities, wholesale, and retail trades (26.8 percent); and fire and business services (17.3 percent) (347). These numbers show that the Puerto Rican population in the United States, despite being one of the earliest to arrive to the United States, has not had the success that other ethnic groups have accomplished.

The most recent Census indicates that Puerto Ricans constitute 8.6 percent of the Hispanic population in this country (U.S. Bureau of the Census 2003, 1) and 66.8 percent of Puerto Ricans 25 years or older have at least a high school education (5). On the other hand, 34.8 percent of Puerto Ricans make $35,000 or more per year and 26.1 percent live in poverty. (U.S. Bureau of the Census 2001, 6).

Data from the 1980 Census showed that half of the Puerto Rican population in the United States was English dominant, one fourth had good skills, and the other fourth had problems with English or did not have any skills in the language (Y. R. Solé 1987, 165–66). On the other hand, the 1990 Census showed that 20 percent of Puerto Ricans claim to be Spanish monolingual. In this community, English language ability is not as strong a determinant of income as it is among other communities such as Mexican-Americans and Cuban-Americans (García 1995).

The linguistic situation of Puerto Ricans in New York City, compared to that of the other two ethnic groups, seems to have certain peculiarities that the literature has captured. In particular, it seems that the Puerto Rican children have a high probability of Spanish language regeneration as adults because they frequently travel to Puerto Rico and because they will have the opportunity to become involved with the large and struggling community of Puerto Rican descent in New York City (García et al. 1988, 496). Zentella (1982) adds to this point by arguing that adults of Puerto Rican descent who stay in the community renew their fluency in Spanish due to the continuous contact with recent in-migrants. Interestingly, these high levels of retention of Spanish among adult Puerto Ricans do not seem to be influenced by identity issues. Zentella (1990c) deals with this topic and reports that 91 percent of the students whom she interviewed have a clear sense of identification regardless of language choice. Moreover, the students claimed that it was possible to be Puerto Rican even if one does not speak Spanish.

Pedraza (1985) provides an argument similar to the ones given by García et al. (1988) and Zentella (1982). He claims that most second-generation Puerto Ricans in New York City do not need to have the Spanish fluency that individuals who were being raised in the same neighborhood between the 1940s and 1960s needed—period when El Barrio's population was growing almost totally from in-migration—because most of their parents and other relatives have some knowledge of English. Despite this difference, he argues that this generation has managed to maintain some fluency in the mother tongue, be it passive or active. The factors that have influenced this maintenance are the constant flow of recent arrivals into the community; the increasing movement of other Hispanics/Latinos into the city; the status of Spanish as a language of stature, with an excellent literary tradition and standardized varieties; the high unemployment rate in the city, which forces many Puerto Ricans to stay in the unskilled service employment sector; and the sense of "collective consciousness" that allows this community to see itself as a national minority. Pedraza gives the idea of a cycle in which society's treatment of this ethnic group and the group's integrity as a speech community work together to keep Spanish use among Puerto Ricans in El Barrio.

Another study is that of Milán (1982), in which he responds to the radical notion that the Spanish spoken in the United States is abnormal or substandard. Milán claims that Puerto Rican Spanish in New York City shows peculiarities largely due to intragroup bilingualism and that this phenomenon is a structural manifestation of a consistent diachronic process (194). His conclusions are mainly based on semantic considerations. Silva-Corvalán (1994, 214) also approaches this issue with regard to the Hispanic/Latino community of Los Angeles, California. She says that language contact speeds up simplification and diffusion of changes, and that the changes manifested in the minority language are already present in the non-contact ancestor variety. She cites the extension of *estar* as one of the examples that illustrates this phenomenon. In addition, she mentions a study by Maandy (1989) which reports a similar situation in the Estonian language among Estonian immigrants in Sweden.

Some authors paint a somewhat different picture of Puerto Ricans in New York City. For instance, Hayden (1966) touches on the issues of elitism, status, and language. The author says that Puerto Ricans show a fluid status hierarchy due to the lack of a well-established elite that can point to its "ancient and honorable" past in the city. This, according to Hayden, makes this hierarchy dependent upon and structured to a degree in the pre-existing framework of the dominant society (191). As a result, and despite the fact that mother tongue is widely regarded as important,

> among Puerto Ricans, who rank next to last in their desire to secure group continuity (compared to other groups of Mexican, Ukrainian and French immigrants), [. . .] language loss may well be welcomed, since it may be taken as a sign of successful assimilation to the general community (196).

Hayden is quick to stress that English is both preferred and used more often than Spanish among spouses, and that "the pressures of the social environment are such that the Puerto Ricans are more likely to rapidly de-emphasize the use of Spanish or its transmission to their own children in connection to most domains of languages" (203).

The following section focuses on census data that will help put in perspective the presence of Cubans, Dominicans, Puerto Ricans, and Hispanics/Latinos in general in the New York City area.

CUBANS, DOMINICANS, AND PUERTO RICANS IN THE NEW YORK CITY AREA: THE 2000 CENSUS

The 2000 Census revealed the facts included in Table 2.1:

Table 2.1 Number of Cubans, Dominicans, and Puerto Ricans living in
New York City according to the 2000 Census

Ethnic origin	*n*	% among Hispanics (*n* = 2,160,554)	% of entire population (*n* = 8,008,278)
Cubans	41,123	1.9	0.5
Dominicans	406,806	18.8	5.0
Puerto Ricans	789,172	36.5	9.8
Other Hispanics	923,453	42.7	11.5
Totals	2,160,554	99.9	26.8

This table indicates that, by far, Puerto Ricans are more represented in
New York City than the other two groups considered in this study.
Dominicans are in second place, followed by Cubans, in third. The table also
reveals the strength that Hispanics/Latinos in general have in this city.
Hispanics/Latinos constitute 26.8 percent of the entire population and
Puerto Ricans alone constitute 9.8 percent. It is important to point out that,
compared with data from the 1990 Census, the Cuban and Puerto Rican
populations decreased 33.7 percent and 15.4 percent, respectively, while the
Dominican and 'Other Hispanics' populations increased 15.8 percent and
40.2 percent, respectively.

Table 2.2 summarizes data about Hudson County, New Jersey. This
county includes West New York, town where subjects—particularly of
Cuban descent—were chosen and interviewed.

In Hudson County, the 'Other Hispanics' group is the most represented, constituting a fifth of the entire population and half of the Hispanic
population. From the three groups considered in this study, Puerto Ricans
are the most represented, followed by Cubans. The difference between the
Cuban and Dominican populations is not extremely significant.
Interestingly, these numbers are considerably different from those obtained
in the previous Census. For instance, the Cuban population decreased 23.2
percent—from 24 percent of the Hispanic population to 14 percent. On the
other hand, the Dominican, Puerto Rican, and 'Other Hispanics' populations increased 40.2 percent, 7.8 percent, and 45.4 percent, respectively.
These facts provide substantial evidence of the growth that the Dominican
group has experienced in recent years.

Table 2.2 Number of Cubans, Dominicans, and Puerto Ricans living in Hudson County, NJ, according to the 2000 census

Ethnic origin	n	% among Hispanics (n = 242,123)	% of entire population (n = 608,975)
Cubans	33,901	14.0	5.6
Dominicans	27,709	11.4	4.6
Puerto Ricans	58,312	24.0	9.6
Other Hispanics	122,201	50.5	20.1
Totals	242,123	99.9	39.9

Specifically in the town of West New York, where most of the subjects from New Jersey live, the ciphers differ notably. Consider table 2.3. It is evident that, in this town, the Hispanic/Latino population is overwhelmingly dominant. Over three fourths of the entire population is of Hispanic/Latino descent and almost half of the population is in the 'Other Hispanics' group. Cubans are the most represented, with close to 25 percent of all Hispanics. This group is followed by Dominicans and Puerto Ricans. Unlike in New York City and Hudson County (as a whole), there are more Dominicans than Puerto Ricans living here. Furthermore, just like in New York City and the entire Hudson County, the Cuban population has decreased in West New York in the last decade (28.2 percent). In fact, Cubans constituted almost half of the Hispanic population in 1990; currently, they constitute approximately one fourth. The Puerto Rican population also decreased (6 percent), whereas the Dominican and 'Other Hispanics' populations increased 40.3 percent and 50.8 percent, respectively.

Table 2.3 Number of Cubans, Dominicans, and Puerto Ricans living in West New York, Hudson County, NJ, according to the 2000 Census

Ethnic origin	n	% among Hispanics (n = 36,038)	% of entire population (n = 45,768)
Cubans	8,991	24.9	19.6
Dominicans	3,847	10.7	8.4
Puerto Ricans	2,791	7.7	6.1
Other Hispanics	20,409	56.6	44.6
Totals	36,038	99.9	78.7

As discussed in chapter one, one of the goals of this study is to compare the speech of first and second-generation Cubans, Dominicans, and Puerto Ricans based on specific phono-phonetic features. In the next section we present the features of Cuban, Dominican, and Puerto Rican Spanish selected for the analysis.

CUBANS, DOMINICANS, AND PUERTO RICANS: DIALECTAL DIFFERENCES

One of the issues with which this study is concerned is that of retention of phono-phonetic features of the mother tongue dialect by members of the second generation. For language is a dynamic system which many times cannot be described 100 percent accurately, and in order to have a measure of comparison, data from first-generation subjects were collected, utilized, and analyzed as well.

The dialects of Spanish spoken by the members of the three ethnic groups included in this study have their own set of phono-phonetic features. For each dialect, three features were selected. They constituted the focus of the phonetic transcription performed to analyze the speech samples of the informants. The following is a summary of the selected features for each dialect, based on the compendium presented by Lipski (1994). In addition, we present findings from studies involving the realization of some of the phonemes in question.

Cuban Spanish

The selected features are:

(1) Devoicing of /rr/. "This is sometimes described as a 'preaspiration' [. . .]; what actually emerges is a sound which is trilled throughout its entire duration, but in which voicing is delayed or totally suppressed" (Lipski 1994, 231)

(2) Neutralization of word- and phrase-final /l/ and /r/. /l/ is more resistant to change. Manifestations (lateralization, deletion, etc.) vary according to sociocultural group and region (Lipski 1994, 231). Guitart (1978) talks about neutralization of /l, r/ in colloquial speech from the educated Havana population. These phonemes produce gemination when followed by a non-coronal consonant. Thus, phrases like 'Mar Caribe' and 'Mal Caribe' become homophones. Lipski also reports retroflexion and glottalization of the first element among the lower socioeconomic strata (232).

(3) Aspiration or complete elision of syllable- and word- final /s/ (232).

Dominican Spanish

From this dialect, the features chosen are:

(1) Neutralization of syllable-final /l/. Loss is growing among the younger generations in Santo Domingo. Realizations range from aspiration, a nasalized aspiration, and a variety of retroflex sounds. In the Cibao region of the northwest, /-l/ may be vocalized to a glide [j]. This is receding due to stigmatization (240–241). In fact, Alba (1988) says that vocalization among the lower classes of Santiago does not reach 30 percent, while it reaches 45 percent among the older generations (12).

(2) Neutralization of syllable-final /r/. This phoneme is more frequently affected than /l/. Elision is overtaking lateralization among the young people of the capital city. Aspiration, nasalized aspiration, and retroflexion are possible realizations. Vocalization of /-r/ is also disappearing (Lipski 1994, 239).

(3) Aspiration or elision of syllable- and word-final /s/. Rates of loss are almost categorical, regardless of level of education (239). According to Sabater (1978, 171), this phenomenon affects the conjugation of verbs in the present indicative, present subjunctive, conditional, and imperfect, especially the 'tú' forms (amas > ama, ames > ame, etc.).

Puerto Rican Spanish

(1) Neutralization of syllable-final /r/. Lateralization is the most common solution. It carries a sociolinguistic stigma and is more common among the lower classes and among older speakers (Lipski 1994, 333).

(2) Velarization of /rr/. It may range from a velar [x] to a uvular trill [R] (333). "There is a preference for velarized /rr/ among the lower classes, among speakers of rural origin, and among male speakers" (334). Morales (1987, 32) supports these conclusions.

(3) Aspiration or elision of syllable- and word-final /s/. "While aspiration is found in all social classes and ages, elision of /s/ appears to have its origins in the capital, and to be spreading outward" (Lipski 1994, 334). Guitart (1978) reports a different realization of /s/ before /p, t, k, b, d, g/. This may lead to assimilation ('los pobres' > 'lo[p]pobre'), and a voiced version may be employed as

well ('lo[b]pobre'). This occurs among young college students from the lower class, who come from towns in the southeastern part of Puerto Rico and now live in Buffalo, NY.

SUMMARY

All in all, most immigrant languages have disappeared in this country. Descendants of most immigrants have been able to maintain identification with their ethnic roots whereas English has supplanted the linguistic code associated with those roots. Politics, policies, immigration rules, and generational factors, among other things, have had a tremendous role in this transition. Hispanics/Latinos and their language have taken a different path. Spanish shows considerable levels of retention across generations. This retention is characterized by extreme variation in both Spanish and English skills. Some of the forces regulating this extreme variation are location, ethnicity, economic and social status, education, values, and perhaps more important, generational differences and age of arrival.

The study we present here sheds more light into the status of the Spanish language among Cubans, Dominicans, and Puerto Ricans living in the New York City area. The next chapter describes the methodology employed in carrying out the study.

Chapter Three
Methodology

This chapter contains a detailed explanation of the research methodology employed in the study carried out. We begin by explaining the rationale underlying the selection of the communities. Then we go on to focus on the field methods utilized and a discussion of the procedures used in the data analysis.

SELECTING THE COMMUNITIES

The city of New York is well known for being the preferred port of entry in the East for immigrants coming to this country. Ethnic communities are many times easily identifiable for groups have often settled in specific parts of the City. This pattern has helped immigrants in several ways. First of all, they are able to socialize and maintain contact with people who share the same cultural and linguistic background. This alleviates the shock that the immigration experience usually involves and allows them to maintain a certain level of psychological connection with the homeland, at least at the beginning. Secondly, they enter into a community that has well-established networks and experience. Immigrants need to know the means to satisfy their basic needs and to obtain basic services, and others who have gone through the experience before become the best aides. Finally, and at a more psychological level, entering into one of these communities guarantees that one will be surrounded by individuals who share the "immigrant" label.

Historically speaking, Cubans, Dominicans, and Puerto Ricans have followed this trend. As it was said in chapter two, Cubans—mainly those arriving after the first immigration wave of the early sixties—settled west of the Hudson River, while Dominicans and Puerto Ricans settled in the Washington Heights and El Barrio sections of Manhattan, respectively. Those were the target communities of this investigation. Some of the subjects lived outside of these communities. However, they have been able to maintain links to the communities, belong to more recent extensions of these communities in other boroughs or parts of the city, and moreover, recognize the importance that the aforementioned communities have in maintaining ethnic values as well as in keeping alive the sense of group.

One relevant criterion for the selection of these communities has to do with what sociologists call 'language-infrastructure.' This concept refers to the language needed to be spoken in a particular community or barrio in order to live and function normally without having to speak English. These three communities have an obvious Spanish language-infrastructure, although this varies depending on the presence of other groups (e.g., African Americans in El Barrio) and on whether social networks incorporate these extra-ethnic groups. Walking through El Barrio and Washington Heights one cannot help but notice the constant use of the Spanish language, the typical *bodegas,* and many other signs that identify the community and those who live there. The same is true in communities west of the Hudson such as Jersey City and West New York. In these communities there is also an abundance of flourishing businesses owned by Cuban Americans.

In sum, we selected the communities for this study based mainly on the immigration patterns of Cubans, Dominicans, and Puerto Ricans, and on the clear vitality that the Spanish language has as a vehicle of communication among members of the community. Because of this, these communities constitute the best sites for a sociolinguistic study of this nature.

FIELD METHODS

There were two key elements in the data collection process needed to complete this study. Subjects completed a questionnaire (see Appendix A and B) and then we recorded a sample of the subjects' vernacular speech in Spanish. The presence of the interviewer has an effect on the quality of such vernacular speech, and many registers and styles are employed throughout the recorded interaction, but the samples used were those that appeared to be least self-monitored.

Subjects Used in the Study

The identification and selection of subjects for this study was primarily based on their ethnic group and by the generation they represented. The other determining issue had to do with several demographic factors, namely, gender, age, and educational level. These factors were strictly controlled to ensure we were dealing with a representative sample. Although statisticians claim that random sampling is the best tool to avoid bias, we opted for stratified sampling. Labov (1966) has addressed some of the problems of the former sampling method, specifically including subjects who do not fulfill the prerequisites of a particular research study.

Initially, we came in contact with prospective subjects through friends who introduced us to them or to someone who, in turn, facilitated contact with them. Afterwards, these subjects introduced us to more prospective subjects with whom they formed social networks (Milroy 1982). Blood, friendship, place of work, or place of residence linked them to each other.

Table 3.1 presents a summary of the number of subjects who participated according to generation, gender, age group, and ethnic group.

Once a subject was selected to participate in the study, and after an informal conversation with us (usually to allay suspicions), the questionnaire was administered. The completion of this questionnaire gave us time to get to know more about each other, and more important, allowed the subjects to become comfortable. These informal conversations continued after the questionnaire was completed. This made the transition between the completion of the questionnaire and the recorded interview a smooth one. Once we started recording the speech sample, the subject was speaking with relative ease and confidence. Subjects were interviewed individually.

The subjects were not told the specific topic of the study. Instead, we introduced ourselves as researchers who were interested in knowing about Cubans, Dominicans, and Puerto Ricans in the New York City area, and told them that some of the questions were related to their Spanish and English skills. Early on in the data collection process we noticed that the use of the term 'linguistics' made subjects want to speak using a more formal style of speech. Therefore, we avoided mentioning this term.

Table 3.1 Number of subjects according to generation, gender, age group, and ethnic group

Generation	First				Second			
Gender	M		F		M		F	
Age Group	1 2 3		1 2 3		1 2 3		1 2 3	
Ethnic Group								Totals
Cubans	2 2 1		2 2 1		2 2 0		2 1 1	= 18
Dominicans	1 2 1		2 2 2		2 2 1		1 2 2	= 20
Puerto Ricans	2 1 2		1 3 1		1 3 1		2 2 1	= 20
								N = 58

M = Male; F = Female; Age Groups: 1 = 20–35; 2 = 36–50; 3 = 51 and above

THE QUESTIONNAIRE

The administered questionnaire served as the instrument for the collection of data, which helped create a sociolinguistic picture of the subjects. This questionnaire was facilitated in Spanish (see Appendix A) and in English (see Appendix B), and subjects were asked to choose the one with which they felt most comfortable based on their linguistic ability.

Questions 1 through 9 provided demographic information and helped classify the subjects. These questions deal with ethnic group, gender, age, place of birth, years lived in the U.S., place of birth of the biological mother and father, and family structure in the home on the thirteenth birthday. This last question was included in order to determine with whom the subject was in contact on a regular basis at a crucial linguistic point in an individual's life. As Labov claims (1984, 29), the most regular speech is that acquired during pre-adolescence and adolescence, when the average individual goes through intense socialization. Furthermore, Lenneberg, in what is known as the Critical Period Hypothesis, argues that the language acquisition device must be stimulated at the right time for it to work successfully. In both its strong and weak versions, the 'right time' is before or during puberty.

Questions 10 and 11 focus on the language(s) used at home on the thirteenth birthday and at the present moment. Questions 12 and 14, on the other hand, focus on the language of instruction at school and the education level attained.[1] Exposure to means of communication—in Spanish and English—is addressed in questions 15 through 18.

The next eight questions seek to find out the subjects' perception of Spanish and English as vehicles for economic progress, and their perception of Spanish as a requisite for membership in their ethnic group and the Hispanic/Latino community at large.

Questions 27 through 34 serve as a self-evaluation of the four skills in Spanish and English. The following eight questions are self-evaluations of their overall skills in both languages compared to those of others, from family members living at home on their thirteenth birthday to other members of the Hispanic/Latino community.

Questions 43 and 44 invite the subject to add more information about their overall skills in both languages. The answers to these questions are not included in the discussion of results. Finally, the last five questions explore linguistic usage in different domains and contexts.

THE INTERVIEW

The majority of the interviews revolved around the following interview modules: traditional foods and customs in the homeland, life in the New

York City area vis-à-vis the homeland, socioeconomic situation in the homeland, jobs, family, and personal experiences. These interview modules gave subjects the opportunity to provide a substantial sample of speech, and moreover, helped them feel comfortable during the interview. We would like to note that most second-generation subjects tended to take the opportunity to speak about these topics to "impress" with all the knowledge they had about the country of origin of their ancestors. We interpreted this as a reflection of their need to reaffirm their identity and their self-perception within the dominant society into which they were born.

DATA ANALYSIS OVERVIEW

This section presents a brief overview of the analytic procedures and instruments used in this investigation. Section one explains how the results provided by the questionnaire and interview—presented in the summary of results sections of chapter four and five—were analyzed and tabulated. Section two describes the tool utilized to identify significant interactions between sociolinguistic factors, and between sociolinguistic factors and the phono-phonetic features of the subjects' speech.

Data Analysis: Summary of Results

The summary of results from the questionnaire and interview did not require any special statistical instrument. Focusing on the questionnaire, the answers to questions 3, 5, 6, 15, and 17 were averaged considering factors such as generation, ethnic group, and age group. For questions 9 and 12, numbers and percentages are given for each possible answer or combination of answers. Answers to questions 10, 11, 14, 16, 18, and 44 through 49 are presented in numbers and percentages, and a scale is presented using the answers available, which describe a continuum of behaviors. Questions 19, 21, 23, 25, and 27 through 42 provided a five-point scale to indicate the answer. These answers were also averaged for specific factors. Answers to open-ended questions such as numbers 20, 22, 24, and 26 are not presented nor commented on. We used these answers, as well as those provided for questions 43 and 44, to better understand the answers to other questions or to be able to explain other aspects of the linguistic behavior of the subject.

Focusing now on the interview, the results are presented in percentages of retention of features. That is, the indicated number represents the percentage of phonetic contexts in which a subject or a particular group—based on the sociolinguistic factors included in the questionnaire—realized the phoneme as the standard allophone and not as the neutralized allophone that characterizes the dialect.

Data Analysis: Analysis of Variance and the SAS Program

The statistical analysis required the consideration of a sub-set of the variables included in the questionnaire. Only twenty-three of the variables were analyzed as dependent variables for the results presented in chapter four. These variables were grouped in five categories, namely, (a) exposure to means of communication; (b) perception of Spanish and English as vehicles for economic progress; (c) perceived relevance of Spanish as a requirement for membership in the ethnic and the Hispanic/Latino communities; (d) self-evaluation of the four major skills in Spanish and English; and (e) domains.

For the results in chapter four, two types of analyses were conducted using the Statistical Analysis Software (= SAS) Program. One-way analyses of variance (= ANOVA) were performed using generation and gender as independent variables—separately—while two-way ANOVAs were performed to explore the interaction of generation and ethnic group, and generation and gender as independent variables.

Two types of analyses were performed using SAS to obtain the results in chapter five. One-way ANOVA was conducted utilizing generation as the independent variable, while two-way ANOVAs were conducted utilizing generation and gender, and generation and ethnic group.[2] The dependent variables in these analyses were the percentages of contexts in which the selected phonemes were realized as their standard Spanish allophone. In the cases of retention of /-l/, /rr/ devoicing, and /rr/ velarization or uvularization, ethnic group was never considered as an independent variable for these phenomena applied to only one of the three groups.

SUMMARY

In this chapter we have described the methodology implemented in the design of this study. The main instruments were a questionnaire and an informal interview. The analysis of data involved the calculation of means and percentages for each of the questions on the questionnaire, as well as for the phoneme retention rates. The analysis also involved the performance of one-way and two-way ANOVAs using the SAS Program. These tests were conducted considering only some of the variables from the questionnaire—in five different groups—and the phoneme retention rates.

In the next chapter we will discuss the results of the questionnaire portion of the study.

Chapter Four
Results: A Sociolinguistic Profile of First- and Second-Generation Speakers of Cuban, Dominican, and Puerto Rican Spanish in the New York City Area

As described in chapters two and three, one of the objectives of this study was to create a sociolinguistic profile of first- and second-generation Cubans, Dominicans, and Puerto Ricans living in the New York City area. This chapter presents the results of the data gathered from the answers provided by the subjects through the questionnaire. The first section includes a summary of the responses; the discussion focuses on specific ethnic groups, the generational factor, and the results of the statistical analysis using SAS.

SUMMARY OF RESPONSES

These results constitute a comparative profile of Cubans, Dominicans, and Puerto Ricans of the first generation vis-à-vis those of the second generation. Results are presented based on the criteria for grouping questionnaire items described in the last chapter.

Demographics

Table 4.1 includes information about the age, years of residence in the United States, and years of residence in the United States before the 13th birthday, according to ethnic group and generation. This table shows that, in every category, Puerto Ricans had the highest average. They show the highest age average, they have more years of residence in the U.S. than Cubans and Dominicans, and they had more years of residence in this country at the time they turned 13 years old. The only exception is found in this last category, specifically within the second-generation group.

Table 4.1 Comparison of first- and second-generation members based on ethnic group, age, years of residence in the U.S., and years of residence in the U.S. at 13th birthday

								Difference		
Generation		First			Second					
Ethnic group		C	D	PR	C	D	PR	C	D	PR
		A*			A*			A*		
AG	1	29.5	28.0	27.7	30.0	26.3	28.7	+0.5	-1.7	+1.0
	2	42.5	40.0	47.8	39.7	38.0	43.0	-2.8	-2.0	-4.8
	3	60.0	58.0	64.7	58.0	54.0	55.0	-2.0	-4.0	-9.7
TG		41.8	41.84	6.8	37.1	39.4	41.1	- 4.7	-2.4	-5.7
		YR*			YR*			YR*		
AG	1	16.8	10.3	9.0	30.0	25.72	8.7	+13.2	+15.4	+19.7
	2	18.8	16.3	36.3	39.7	38.00	43.0	+20.9	+21.7	+6.7
	3	17.5	17.7	47.7	58.0	54.00	55.0	+40.5	+36.3	+7.3
G	1	7.7	14.9	31.5	37.1	39.20	41.1	+19.4	+24.3	+9.6
		YR13*			YR13*					
AG	1	1.8	0.0	0.0	13.0	12.3	13.0	+11.2	+12.3	+13.0
	2	0.0	0.5	5.3	13.0	13.0	13.0	+13.0	+12.5	+7.7
	3	0.0	0.0	2.3	13.0	13.0	13.0	+13.0	+13.0	+10.7
TG		0.7	0.2	2.8	13.0	12.8	13.0	+12.3	+12.6	+10.2

* Results are given in averages.
C = Cubans; D = Dominicans; PR = Puerto Ricans
A = Age; YR = Years of Residence in The U.S.; YR13 = Years of Residence in the U.S. before 13th birthday
G = Age group: 1 = 20–35; 2 = 36–50; 3 = 51 and over
TG = Total group

The first-generation subjects averaged 43.1 years of age, i.e., 3.7 years more than the second-generation. In terms of the years of residence in the United States, the subjects from the first generation averaged 21.4 years, while the subjects from the second generation had an average of 39.3 years, 17.9 years more than their first-generation counterpart. Finally, first-generation members lived an average of 1.2 years in the U.S. before their 13th birthday, as opposed to 12.97 years for the second-generation members (11.8 years more). The average age for the second-generation members was not 13 years because one of the Dominican subjects had lived in the Dominican Republic for two years.

Table 4.2 provides information about the place of birth, place of birth of the mother, and place of birth of the father of the Cuban subjects according to generation.

Table 4.2 Comparison of first- and second-generation Cuban subjects based on place of birth, place of birth of the mother, and place of birth of the father

Generation			First		Second
			PB*		PB*
AG	1	Cuba	100% (4/4)	NYA	75% (3/4)
				ONYA	25% (1/4)
	2	Cuba	100% (4/4)	NYA	100% (3/3)
	3	Cuba	100% (2/2)	NYA	100% (1/1)
TG		Cuba	100% (10/10)	NYA	88% (7/8)
				ONYA	13% (1/8)
			PBM*		PBM*
AG	1	Cuba	100% (4/4)	Cuba	100% (4/4)
	2	Cuba	100% (4/4)	Cuba	100% (3/3)
	3	Cuba	50% (1/2)	Cuba	100% (1/1)
		Africa	50% (1/2)		
TG		Cuba	90% (9/10)	Cuba	100% (8/8)
		Africa	10% (1/10)		
			PBF*		PBF*
AG	1	Cuba	100% (4/4)	Cuba	50% (2/4)
				Mexico	25% (1/4)
				ONYA	25% (1/4)
	2	Cuba	75% (3/4)	Cuba	100% (3/3)
		Venezuela	25% (1/4)		
	3	Cuba	50% (1/2)	Cuba	100% (1/1)
		Africa	50% (1/2)		
TG		Cuba	80% (8/10)	Cuba	75% (6/8)
		Venezuela	10% (1/10)	Mexico	13% (1/8)
		Africa	10% (1/10)	ONYA	13% (1/8)

* Results are given in percentages. These percentages are rounded out.
PB = Place of birth; PBM = Place of birth of the mother; PBF = Place of birth of the father
AG = Age group: 1 = 20–35; 2 = 36–50; 3 = 51 and over
TG = Total group
ONYA = Outside of the New York area (in the U.S.)

One hundred percent of the first-generation Cubans were born in Cuba. Ninety percent of their mothers were born in Cuba as well; one of them—10 percent—was born in Africa. With regards to their fathers, 80 percent were born in Cuba, 10 percent in Venezuela, and 10 percent in Africa.

Out of the 8 second-generation Cubans in the study, 88 percent were born in the New York City area and 13 percent outside of this area. All of their mothers were born in Cuba, as well as 75 percent of their fathers. Of the fathers, 13 percent were born in Mexico and 13 percent outside of the New York area.

The information about the place of birth, place of birth of the mother, and place of birth of the father of the Dominican subjects is included in table 4.3.

All of the first-generation Dominicans, their mothers, and their fathers were born in the Dominican Republic. Ninety percent of the second-generation Dominicans were born in the New York area; 10 percent of them were born outside of the area. Ninety percent of their mothers and 100 percent of their fathers were born in the Dominican Republic. Of the mothers, 10 percent were born in the U.S, outside of the New York City area.

Table 4.4 presents the information about the place of birth, place of birth of the mother, and place of birth of the father of the Puerto Rican subjects. All the first-generation Puerto Ricans were born in Puerto Rico, as well as their fathers and 90 percent of their mothers. The remaining 10 percent of the mothers were born in the New York area. One hundred percent of the second-generation Puerto Ricans were born in the New York area. Ten percent of the mothers were born there too. Ninety percent of the mothers and 100 percent of the fathers were born in Puerto Rico.

All the first-generation subjects were born in their country of origin, which was a requirement for participation in the study. While 93 percent of the second-generation subjects were born in the New York City area, 7 percent were born outside of the area. These two subjects, however, have lived in the area for a considerable number of years and are well integrated in the community. The great majority of the subjects' parents were born in their countries of origin, followed by the United States. Parents born in the U.S. who married first-generation immigrants and their children were considered for the study. One first-generation subject's mother was born in the New York City area but she had grown up in a linguistically isolated household, and moreover, she married a first-generation immigrant from her country of origin. Another first-generation subject's parents were born in Africa and moved to Cuba before the subject's birth. The same applies to another subject's father, who was born in Venezuela and later moved to and married in Cuba. Finally, the

Table 4.3 Comparison of first- and second-generation Dominican subjects based on place of birth, place of birth of the mother, and place of birth of the father

Generation			First			Second	
			PB*			PB*	
AG	1	DR	100% (3/3)		NYA	100% (3/3)	
	2	DR	100% (4/4)		NYA	100% (4/4)	
	3	DR	100% (3/3)		NYA	67% (2/3)	
					ONYA	33% (1/3)	
TG		DR	100% (10/10)		NYA	90% (9/10)	
					ONYA	10% (1/10)	
			PBM*			PBM*	
AG	1	DR	100% (3/3)		DR	100% (3/3)	
	2	DR	100% (4/4)		DR	100% (4/4)	
	3	DR	100% (3/3)		DR	67% (2/3)	
					ONYA	33% (1/3)	
TG		DR	100% (10/10)		DR	90% (9/10)	
					ONYA	10% (1/10)	
			PBF*			PBF*	
AG	1	DR	100% (3/3)		DR	100% (3/3)	
	2	DR	100% (4/4)		DR	100% (4/4)	
	3	DR	100% (3/3)		DR	100% (3/3)	
TG		DR	100% (10/10)		DR	100% (10/10)	

* Results are given in percentages. These percentages are rounded out.
PB = Place of birth; PBM = Place of birth of the mother; PBF = Place of birth of the father
AG = Age group: 1 = 20–35; 2 = 36–50; 3 = 51 and over
TG = Total group
DR = Dominican Republic; NYA = New York area; ONYA = Outside of the New York area (in the U.S.)

father of a member of the second generation was born in Mexico, married the subject's mother in the United States, but never lived in the same household. This fact did not disqualify this subject.

Table 4.5 describes the family constitution at the point when the subjects turned 13 years old. The categories presented were created based on the combinations of answers to question 9 provided by the subjects. As we can see, most of the subjects lived with their nuclear families at the time they turned 13 years old. This fact does not vary from generation to generation.

Table 4.4 Comparison of first- and second-generation Puerto Rican subjects based on place of birth, place of birth of the mother, and place of birth of the father

Generation			First		Second	
			PB*		PB*	
AG	1	PR	100% (3/3)	NYA	100% (3/3)	
	2	PR	100% (4/4)	NYA	100% (5/5)	
	3	PR	100% (3/3)	NYA	100% (2/2)	
TG		PR	100% (10/10)	NYA	100% (10/10)	
			PBM*		PBM*	
AG	1	PR	67% (2/3)	PR	100% (3/3)	
		NYA	33% (1/3)			
	2	PR	100% (4/4)	PR	100% (5/5)	
	3	PR	100% (3/3)	PR	50% (1/2)	
		NYA	50%(1/2)			
TG		PR	90% (9/10)	PR	90% (9/10)	
		NYA	10% (1/10)	NYA	10% (1/10)	
			PBF*		PBF*	
AG	1	PR	100% (3/3)	PR	100% (3/3)	
	2	PR	100% (4/4)	PR	100% (5/5)	
	3	PR	100% (3/3)	PR	100% (2/2)	
	TG	PR	100% (10/10)	PR	100% (10/10)	

* Results are given in percentages. These percentages are rounded out.
PB = Place of birth; PBM = Place of birth of the mother; PBF = Place of birth of the father
AG = Age group: 1 = 20–35; 2 = 36–50; 3 = 51 and over
TG = Total group
PR = Puerto Rico; NYA = New York area; ONYA = Outside of the New York area (in the U.S.)

Dominicans have the highest percentages of individuals who lived in this type of family on their 13th birthday, both in the first generation and the second generation. The second most common family type varies from group to group, but in two out of the six groups, 'nuclear families with other relatives' is the second most common one.

LANGUAGE(S) OF THE HOME

The following is a comparison of the language(s) of the home on the 13th birthday and the language(s) of the home now for the subjects from the three

Table 4.5 Comparison of first- and second-generation Cubans, Dominicans, and Puerto Ricans based on family constitution on 13th birthday

Generation			First			Second		
Ethnic group			C	D	PR	C	D	PR
		FC13*						
AG	1	N	33%	33%	33%	25%	67%	
		N+		33%			25%	33%
		N++						
		N-	33%	33%	33%			
		NX		33%	33%	25%		67%
		N-O						
		O						
		R				25%		33%
	2	N	50%	75%	50%	67%	50%	80%
		N+	25%	25%	25%		25%	
		N++	25%					
		N-						
		NX						
		N-O						
		O						
		R			25%	33%	25%	20%
	3	N	50%	100%	33%		33%	
		N+					33%	100%
		N++					33%	
		N-						
		NX			33%			
		N-O	50%					
		O				100%		
		R			33%			
TG		N	40%	70%	40%	38%	50%	40%
		N+	30%	10%	10%	13%	30%	20%
		N++	10%				10%	
		N-	10%	10%	10%			
		NX		10%	20%	13%		20%
		N-O	10%					
		O				13%		
		R			20%	25%	10%	20%

* Results are given in percentages. These percentages are rounded out.
C = Cubans; D = Dominicans; PR = Puerto Ricans
FC13 = Family constitution on 13th birthday
AG = Age group: 1 = 20–35; 2 = 36–50; 3 = 51 and over
TG = Total group
N = Nuclear family; N+ = Nuclear family plus other relatives; N++ = Nuclear family plus other non-relatives; N- = Nuclear family with one stepparent;
NX =Nuclear family with a single parent; N-O = Nuclear family, one stepparent, and other people; O = Other people; R = Relatives.

ethnic groups. Questions 10 and 11 provided five choices (letters), each one describing a linguistic behavior: A = Spanish only; B = Mostly Spanish; C = Both Spanish and English; D = Mostly English; and E = English only. (See Appendices.) Each answer received a numerical value (A = 1, B = 2, C = 3, D = 4, and E = 5), these values were added up, and an average was obtained. Thus, the averages presented in this table represent the average language choice—average of points in the scale—for the age groups and generational groups.

As we can see in Table 4.6, among the first-generation members, Dominicans had the lowest average for language(s) of the home at age 13 (1, "Spanish only") and for language(s) of the home now (2, "mostly Spanish"). Puerto Ricans had the highest average for the first category (1.3, between "Spanish only" and "mostly Spanish"). Cubans had the highest average for the second category (2.6, between "mostly Spanish," and "both Spanish and English"). There are no great differences between the averages for these categories.

Dominicans also had the lowest averages for these categories among their second-generation members: 1.1 (between "Spanish only" and "mostly Spanish") and 2.7 (between "mostly Spanish," and "both Spanish and English"), respectively. Puerto Ricans had the highest average for the first category (3, "both Spanish and English"), and Cubans had the highest one for the second one (3.5, between "both Spanish and English," and "mostly English"). Again, there are no great differences between the averages for these categories.

One can confirm that the tendency is for an individual, be it from the first generation or the second generation, to use more English than what was used when they were 13 years old, as the movement on the scale shows (see bottom of the table). All the ethnic groups and generations showed an increase except for the second-generation Puerto Ricans from age group 3, who showed no change at all. This means that the current first generation is providing their offspring—the second generation of the future—with a home environment in which the English language is used more frequently than when they were growing up. If the trend is movement towards higher averages on the scale one can predict the answers that the second generation of the future will provide, that is, even more use of English in the home environment.

Overall, the average for the language spoken at home at the point when they turned 13 years old among first-generation members was 1.2 (between the categories of "Spanish only" and "mostly Spanish"). Among second-generation members, on the other hand, the average was exactly 2

Table 4.6 Comparison of first- and second-generation Cubans, Dominicans, and Puerto Ricans based on the language(s) spoken at home on their 13th birthday and the language(s) spoken at home now

Generation		First			Second			Difference		
Ethnic group		C	D	PR	C	D	PR	C	D	PR
		LH13*			LH13*			LH13*		
AG	1	1.3	1.0	1.0	1.8	1.0	3.0	+0.5	0.0	+2.0
	2	1.0	1.0	1.5	1.7	1.0	2.6	+0.7	0.0	+1.1
	3	1.5	1.0	1.3	4.0	1.3	4.0	+2.5	+0.3	+2.7
TG		1.2	1.0	1.3	2.0	1.1	3.0	+0.8	+0.1	+1.7
		LHN*			LHN*			LHN*		
AG	1	2.8	1.7	2.7	3.5	2.0	3.3	+0.7	+0.3	+0.6
	2	2.3	2.0	2.8	3.0	3.0	3.2	+0.7	+1.0	+0.4
	3	3.0	2.3	1.7	5.0	3.0	4.0	+2.0	+0.7	+2.3
TG		2.6	2.0	2.4	3.5	2.7	3.4	+0.9	+0.7	+1.0

Difference (LHN–LH13)										
AG	1	+1.5	+0.7	+1.7	+1.7	+1.0	+0.3			
	2	+1.3	+1.0	+1.3	+1.3	+2.0	+0.6			
	3	+1.5	+1.3	+0.4	+1.0	+1.7	0.0			
TG		+1.4	+1.0	+1.1	+1.5	+1.6	+0.4			

* Results given are averages of points in the following scale:
1 = Spanish only; 2 = Mostly Spanish; 3 = Both Spanish and English;
4 = Mostly English; 5 = English only.
C = Cubans; D = Dominicans; PR = Puerto Ricans
LH13 = Language of the home on the 13th birthday; LHN = Language of the home now
AG = Age group: 1 = 20–35; 2 = 36–50; 3 = 51 and over
TG = Total group

("mostly Spanish"), with .8 points more. This movement on the scale was more evident in age group 3, subjects who—based on their average age, 55.2 years old—turned thirteen 42.2 years ago. According to the scale, they averaged 2.5 points more than their first-generation counterparts.

First-generation members averaged 2.6 in terms of the language spoken at home now (between "mostly Spanish," and "both Spanish and English").

Second-generation members averaged 3.5 (between "mostly Spanish and English," and "mostly English"). Once again, when we compare the first generation with the second generation, the movement is towards less use of Spanish and more use of English in the home environment in the second generation. Second-generation members from age group 3 showed a movement of two points on the scale compared to the same group of the first generation.

LANGUAGE(S) OF INSTRUCTION AND EDUCATIONAL LEVEL ATTAINED

Table 4.7 presents a summary of the education—up to the high school level—received by the subjects, characterized by the language(s) in which instruction was administered. They had to choose the answer that included the language(s) of instruction used most of the time while they attended school in their country of origin or in the U.S. The table only includes those answers selected by the subjects.

Most of the first-generation members, regardless of ethnic group, received instruction in Spanish, followed by instruction in English. Percentages are higher among Cubans and Dominicans. None of the second-generation members received instruction in Spanish. Most of these subjects received instruction in English. Percentages are higher among Cubans.

The educational level attained by the subjects is illustrated in table 4.8. The choices provided for this question make up a continuum, from "no high school diploma" to "college diploma."[1] Specifically, A = no high school diploma, B = High school diploma, C = Some college education (did not graduate), D = Associate Degree, E = College Degree (B.A. or graduate school).[2] These choices were assigned a numerical value (A = 1, B = 2, C = 3, D = 4, and E = 5), these values were added up and averaged out to obtain a representative value for specific groups. The numbers in the table, thus, represent an approximation to one alternative or the other, an average of points in the scale.

Dominicans attained the highest level of education of all the first-generation groups, with an average of 3.7 (between "some college education (did not graduate)" and "Associate Degree"). Puerto Ricans attained the lowest, with 2.7—between "high school diploma" and "some college education (did not graduate)." Among the second-generation members, Cubans attained the highest level of education. The average was 3.5—between "some college education (did not graduate)" and "Associate Degree." The lowest average for this group was obtained by Dominicans, with 2.8—between "high school diploma" and "some college education (did not graduate)."

If we only consider the generational factor we notice that there are no differences in the educational level attained by both cohorts. Both groups

Table 4.7 Comparison of first- and second-generation Cubans, Dominicans, and Puerto Ricans based on the language(s) of instruction received

Generation			First			Second		
Ethnic group			C	D	PR	C	D	PR
				LI*			LI*	
AG	1	S	50%	67%	100%			
		E	25%			100%	67%	100%
		B						
		BE	25%	33%			33%	
	2	S	75%	50%	25%			
		E	25%	25%	75%	100%	100%	80%
		B		25%				
		BE						20%
	3	S	100%	100%	67%			
		E			33%	100%	100%	100%
		B						
		BE						
TG		S	70%	70%	60%			
		E	20%	20%	40%	100%	90%	90%
		B		10%				
		BE	10%				10%	10%

* Results are given in percentages. These percentages are rounded out.
C = Cubans; D = Dominicans; PR = Puerto Ricans
LI = Language of instruction
AG = Age group: 1 = 20–35; 2 = 36–50; 3 = 51 and over
TG = Total group
S = (Mostly) Spanish; E = (Mostly) English; B = Both languages (Bilingual Education);
BE = Bilingual Education followed by (mostly) English

averaged 3.2 on the scale (between "high school diploma" and "some college education"). The main reason for this is that we selected participants with different backgrounds and from different social strata. While some subjects had not completed high school, others had completed graduate studies in various fields. This applies to subjects from the three ethnic groups included in this investigation. In our opinion, this is a great advantage of the study: it considers the opinions and speech samples of individuals from a variety of backgrounds who share significant characteristics, namely, ethnicity and belonging to a particular generational group.

Table 4.8 Comparison of first- and second-generation Cubans, Dominicans, and Puerto Ricans based on their attained educational level

								Difference		
Generation		First			Second					
Ethnic group		C	D	PR	C	D	PR	C	D	PR
			ELA*			ELA*			ELA*	
AG	1	3.3	4.3	3.7	3.3	3.3	3.0	0.0	-1.0	-0.7
	2	3.3	4.3	3.0	3.3	2.8	3.4	0.0	-1.5	+0.4
	3	3.0	2.3	1.3	5.0	2.3	3.5	+2.0	0.0	+2.2
TG		3.2	3.7	2.7	3.5	2.8	3.3	+0.3	-0.9	+0.6

* Results given are averages of points in the following scale:
1 = No high school diploma; 2 = High school diploma; 3 = Some college education (did not graduate); 4 = Associate Degree; 5 = College diploma (B.A. or graduate school).
C = Cubans; D = Dominicans; PR = Puerto Ricans
ELA = Educational level attained
AG = Age group: 1 = 20–35; 2 = 36–50; 3 = 51 and over
TG = Total group

EXPOSURE TO MEANS OF COMMUNICATION

Table 4.9 illustrates how many hours per week the subjects are exposed to Spanish- and English-language radio and music. The numbers presented are averages of hours that the particular group listens to Spanish- and English-language radio and music.

In the first-generation group, Cubans had the highest average of hours per week for listening to Spanish-language radio and music (23.6 hours). Dominicans had the lowest, with 2.6 hours. Puerto Ricans had the highest average for listening to English-language radio and music, with 8.8 hours. Dominicans had the lowest, with 6.7 hours.

Among the second-generation members, Dominicans listen to Spanish-language radio and music more (15.6 hours), while Puerto Ricans listen to it less than the other groups (8.8 hours). Puerto Ricans, however, listen to English-language radio and music more than others (20.1 hours). Cubans listen to it less than the other two groups (17.6 hours). The average of hours per week spent listening to Spanish-language radio and music decreases in the second-generation, whereas the average of hours listening to English-language radio and music increases.

Let us consider how many hours per week the subjects are exposed to Spanish- and English-language TV. The results are included in table 4.10.

Table 4.9 Comparison of first- and second-generation Cubans, Dominicans, and Puerto Ricans based on their exposure to Spanish- and English-language radio and music

Generation		First			Second			Difference		
Ethnic group		C	D	PR	C	D	PR	C	D	PR
		SRM*			SRM*			SRM*		
AG	1	22.3	3.3	3.0	7.0	2.2	10.7	-15.3	-1.1	+7.7
	2	28.0	3.4	25.9	19.3	28.5	9.8	-8.7	+25.1	-16.1
	3	17.5	4.0	15.3	0.0	11.7	3.5	-17.5	+7.7	-11.8
TG		23.6	2.6	15.9	10.8	15.6	8.8	-12.8	+13.0	-7.1
		ERM*			ERM*			ERM*		
AG	1	14.0	11.0	7.5	20.6	23.3	43.0	+6.6	+12.3	+35.5
	2	5.0	6.5	13.8	16.0	16.8	11.4	+11.0	+10.3	-2.4
	3	2.5	2.7	3.3	10.0	13.3	7.3	+7.5	+10.6	+4.0
TG		8.1	6.7	8.8	17.6	17.7	20.1	+9.5	+11.0	+11.3

* Results are given in average of hours per week.
C = Cubans; D = Dominicans; PR = Puerto Ricans
SRM = Spanish radio and music; ERM = English radio and music
AG = Age group: 1 = 20–35; 2 = 36–50; 3 = 51 and over
TG = Total group

The numbers included in the table are averages of hours per week. Cubans watch more Spanish-language TV than any other first-generation group (22.9 hours per week). Dominicans watch the least, with 9.8 hours per week. Puerto Ricans watch 19.2 hours of English-language TV, more than any other group. Dominicans watch 10.3 hours, less than any other group. Among the second generation, Dominicans watch more Spanish-language TV, with 10.5 hours. Cubans watch the least, 3.4 hours. Puerto Ricans, on the other hand, watch more English-language TV, 25.8 hours per week. Cubans watch 17.6 hours, being the group that watches the least. In this category it is not possible to say that viewing in Spanish decreases in the second generation and that English viewing increases, since there is considerable variation across age groups.

Table 4.11 compares how often the subjects read Spanish- and English-language newspapers and magazines. This question provided answers that form a continuum (A = Daily, B = Several times a week, C = Once a week, D = Several times a week, E = About once a month, F = Less than once a

Table 4.10 Comparison of first- and second-generation Cubans, Dominicans, and Puerto Ricans based on their exposure to Spanish- and English-language TV

								Difference		
Generation		First			Second					
Ethnic group		C	D	PR	C	D	PR	C	D	PR
		STV*			STV*			STV*		
AG	1	11.8	10.7	6.7	2.5	3.0	10.0	-9.3	-7.7	+3.3
	2	24.3	10.0	3.0	5.7	12.8	2.2	-18.6	+2.8	-0.8
	3	42.3	8.7	25.3	0.0	15.0	0.0	-42.3	+6.3	- 25.3
TG		22.9	9.8	10.8	3.4	10.5	4.1	-19.5	+0.7	+0.7
		ETV*			ETV*			ETV*		
AG	1	24.0	15.7	22.7	14.5	18.0	21.0	-9.5	+2.3	-2.7
	2	12.5	10.8	22.0	21.0	27.3	30.0	+8.5	+16.5	+8.0
	3	12.5	4.3	12.0	20.0	21.3	22.5	+7.5	+17.0	+10.5
	TG	17.1	10.3	19.2	17.6	22.7	25.8	+0.5	+12.4	+6.6

* Results are given in average of hours per week.
C = Cubans; D = Dominicans; PR = Puerto Ricans
STV = Spanish TV; ETV = English TV
AG = Age group: 1 = 20–35; 2 = 36–50; 3 = 51 and over
TG = Total group

month, and G = Never). These letters were given numerical values (A = 1, B = 2, etc.) and an average was calculated. The numbers presented refer to an average of points on this scale. Cubans, Dominicans, and Puerto Ricans from the first generation read Spanish newspapers and magazines between "several times a week" and "once a week," with averages of 2.6, 2.9, and 2.9, respectively. There is variation, however, when it comes to reading English newspapers and magazines. Puerto Ricans read them with the same frequency (2.4 points), Cubans read them between "once a week" and "several times a week" (3.5 points), and Dominicans read them between "several times a month" and "about once a month." Thus, first-generation Puerto Ricans are exposed to English-language written forms of communication more often than the first-generation members of the other ethnic groups. Dominicans are exposed to them less than the other groups.

Cubans, Dominicans, and Puerto Ricans from the second generation read Spanish newspapers and magazines between "about once a month" and "less than once a month." The averages were 5.4, 5.3, and 5.9, respectively. Cubans read English newspapers and magazines between "daily" and

Table 4.11 Comparison of first- and second-generation Cubans, Dominicans, and Puerto Ricans based on how often they read Spanish- and English-language newspapers and magazines

Generation		First			Second			Difference		
Ethnic group		C	D	PR	C	D	PR	C	D	PR
		SNM*			SNM*			SNM*		
AG	1	3.3	3.7	2.7	5.3	5.7	6.3	+2.0	+2.0	+3.6
	2	2.3	3.0	2.8	5.3	6.0	5.2	+2.0	+3.0	+2.4
	3	2.0	2.0	3.3	6.0	4.0	7.0	+4.0	+2.0	+3.7
TG		2.6	2.9	2.9	5.4	5.3	5.9	+2.8	+2.4	+3.0
		ENM*			ENM*			ENM*		
AG	1	3.0	5.0	1.3	1.5	3.3	3.3	-1.5	-1.7	+2.0
	2	4.3	4.0	2.8	2.0	3.3	2.4	-2.3	-0.7	-0.4
	3	3.0	5.0	3.0	1.0	2.3	2.0	-2.0	-2.7	-1.0
TG		3.5	4.6	2.4	1.6	3.0	2.6	-1.9	-1.6	+0.6

* Results are given in averages of points in the following scale:
1 = Daily; 2 = Several times a week; 3 = Once a week; 4 = Several times a month; 5 = About once a month; 6 = Less than once a month; 7 = Never.
C = Cubans; D = Dominicans; PR = Puerto Ricans
SNM = Spanish newspapers and magazines; ENM = English newspapers and magazines
AG = Age group: 1 = 20–35; 2 = 36–50; 3 = 51 and over
TG = Total group

"several times a week" (1.6 points), Puerto Ricans read them between "several times a week" and "once a week" (2.6 points), and Dominicans read them between "once a week" and "several times a month" (3 points). This means that second-generation Cubans are exposed to English-language written forms of communication more than any other ethnic group from the second generation.

One interesting finding is that first-generation members read in the English language more often than second-generation members read in Spanish (with a difference of 2 points on the scale). This shows that the process that involves frequently reading in English starts in the first generation.

With regards to exposure to means of communication, there are four statistically significant differences determined by generational differences.[3] These differences are in the hours spent watching both Spanish- (p < .0106) and English-language TV (p < .0001), in the hours spent listening to English-language radio and music (p < .0242), and in the frequency with which the subjects read Spanish-language newspapers and magazines (p < .0001). In other words, members from the first generation watch significantly more Spanish-language TV and read Spanish-language newspapers and magazines significantly more than members from the second generation. The latter group, on the other hand, watches significantly more English-language TV and listens to English-language radio and music significantly more than the former group. There are no significant differences in the number of hours spent listening to Spanish-language radio and music (p < .6635). Second-generation members are exposed to this medium of communication with a frequency that compares to that of first-generation members. Furthermore, there were no significant differences in the frequency with which the subjects read English-language newspapers and magazines (p < .0571). Thus, Spanish radio and music provide second-generation members with a connection to the Spanish language. This medium seems to be preferred over television and written means of communication in Spanish. On the contrary, English-language written means of communication are preferred over radio and music, and TV among first-generation members. Newspapers and magazines in English appeal to first-generation individuals when it comes to being exposed to means of communication in this language, more than any other.

The only significant statistical difference for gender and exposure to means of communication was found in the frequency with which the subjects read English- language newspapers and magazines (p < .0068). In general, males read them more frequently (between "several times a week" and "once a week") than women (between "once a week" and "several times a month"). There were no significant differences regarding hours spent listening to radio and music in both languages (p < .3774 for Spanish and .4011 for English), in hours spent watching TV in both languages (p < .1642 for Spanish and .1570 for English), and frequency with which males and females read Spanish-language newspapers and magazines (p < .9385).

Generation and ethnic group only yielded one significant difference: Spanish-language radio and music (p < .0163). This may be attributable to the relatively low frequency with which first-generation Dominicans are exposed to it and to the relatively high frequency with which first-generation Cubans are exposed to it. The remaining four sub-groups obtained very similar means. Generation and gender, on the other hand, showed significance in determining differences regarding English-language newspapers and magazines (p < .0083). Particularly, the frequency with which females and males read English-language newspapers and magazines increases significantly among the second generation. First-generation females read them between "several times a month" and "once a month," while second-generation females read them between "several times a week" and "once a week." First-generation and second-generation males, however, read them between "several times a week" and "once a week." There is no increase among males.

Perception of Spanish and English as Vehicles for Economic Progress

Table 4.12 presents the results of the questions regarding the subjects' opinion about the relevance of Spanish and English as vehicles for economic progress. The numbers included in this table are averages of the numeric values in a five-point scale in which 1 = Not necessary at all and 5 = Extremely necessary.

This table suggests that, among first-generation members, Cubans and Dominicans have a higher regard for Spanish as a vehicle for economic progress. Their averages were 4.4 points and 4.1 points, respectively, that is, between "very necessary" and "extremely necessary." Puerto Ricans follow with 3.6 points (between "necessary" and "very necessary").

Table 4.12 Comparison of first- and second-generation Cubans, Dominicans, and Puerto Ricans based on their perception of Spanish and English as vehicles for economic progress

								Difference		
Generation		First			Second					
Ethnic group		C	D	PR	C	D	PR	C	D	PR
			SEP*			SEP*			SEP*	
AG	1	4.3	5.0	4.3	5.0	4.3	3.7	0.0	-0.7	-0.6
	2	4.3	3.5	3.0	4.3	4.5	4.0	0.0	+1.0	+1.0
	3	5.0	4.0	3.7	3.0	3.0	4.5	-2.0	-1.0	+0.8
TG		4.4	4.1	3.6	4.5	4.0	4.0	+0.1	-0.1	+0.4
			EEP*			EEP*			EEP*	
AG	1	5.0	4.7	5.0	5.0	5.0	4.7	0.0	+0.3	-0.3
	2	5.0	4.8	5.0	5.0	5.0	4.8	0.0	+0.2	-0.2
	3	5.0	5.0	5.0	5.0	5.0	5.0	0.0	0.0	0.0
TG		5.0	4.8	5.0	5.0	5.0	4.8	0.0	+0.2	-0.2

* Results are given in averages of points in the following scale: 1 = Not necessary at all; 2 = Somewhat necessary; 3 = Necessary; 4 = Very necessary; 5 = Extremely necessary.
C = Cubans; D = Dominicans; PR = Puerto Ricans
SEP = Spanish as a vehicle for (economic) progress; EEP = English as a vehicle for (economic) progress
AG = Age group: 1 = 20–35; 2 = 36–50; 3 = 51 and over
TG = Total group

First-generation Cubans and Dominicans also have the highest regard for English as a vehicle for economic progress, with averages of 5 points ("extremely necessary"). Puerto Ricans are not too far behind with 4.8 points (between "very necessary" and "extremely necessary").

The situation is somewhat similar among second-generation members. Cubans have the highest regard for Spanish with 4.5 (between "very necessary" and "extremely necessary"), followed by Dominicans and Puerto Ricans with 4 points ("very necessary"). Cubans and Dominicans have the same kind of regard for English in this category, with 5 points ("extremely necessary"). Puerto Ricans averaged 4.8 points (between "very necessary" and "extremely necessary").

There are no statistically significant differences in the importance first-generation and second-generation individuals attribute to Spanish (p < .6321) and English (p < .9442) for economic advancement in New York City. As said before, both first-generation and second-generation members perceive both languages between "very necessary" and "extremely necessary" (for first-generation members, Spanish is "very necessary"). In fact, both groups had a mean of 4.9 (where 5 = "extremely necessary") for English, for obvious reasons. When it comes to gender differences, women consider English more important than men (p < .0322). The importance females and males attribute to Spanish is not significant (p < .2384).

Differences were also found in the category of perception of English as a vehicle for economic progress and the combination of generation and ethnic group (p < .0468). In this case, the differences were determined by first-generation Cubans and second-generation Puerto Ricans. The other four sub-groups had a mean of 5 ("extremely necessary"). This is surprising because Puerto Ricans were the first ones to immigrate into this country and they definitely had to survive without the laws and sensitivity that guarantee better treatment towards immigrants today. The group of second-generation Puerto Ricans is the oldest cohort of Puerto Ricans in this city and one would expect them to remember the advantages of knowing English to advance economically here when evaluating its importance. The generation and gender variables did not show any statistical significance.

Perceived Relevance of Spanish as a Requirement for Membership in the Ethnic Community and in the Hispanic/Latino Community

The purpose of table 4.13 is to compare the opinions of the subjects regarding the perceived relevance of the Spanish language as a requirement for membership in the ethnic community and in the Hispanic/Latino community in general. Subjects indicated their answers using a five-point scale

Table 4.13 Comparison of first- and second-generation Cubans, Dominicans, and Puerto Ricans based on the perceived relevance of Spanish for membership in their communities and in the Hispanic/Latino community

								Difference		
Generation		First			Second					
Ethnic group		C	D	PR	C	D	PR	C	D	PR
		SMC*			SMC*			SMC*		
AG	1	4.8	4.5	2.3	3.8	5.0	3.7	-1.0	+0.5	+1.4
	2	4.8	4.8	3.5	5.0	4.8	4.0	+0.2	0.0	+0.5
	3	5.0	4.7	3.7	3.0	3.7	3.0	-2.0	-1.0	-0.7
TG		4.8	4.7	3.2	4.1	4.5	3.7	-0.7	-0.2	+0.5
		SMHLC*			SMHLC*			SMHLC*		
AG	1	4.8	4.5	3.7	4.0	2.3	4.0	-0.8	-2.2	+0.3
	2	4.3	4.0	4.5	5.0	4.5	4.8	+0.7	+0.5	+0.3
	3	5.0	4.7	3.7	3.0	3.7	3.0	-2.0	-1.0	-0.7
TG		4.6	4.3	4.0	4.3	3.6	4.2	-0.3	-0.7	+0.2

* Results are given in averages of points in the following scale: 1 = Not necessary at all; 2 = Somewhat necessary; 3 = Necessary; 4 = Very necessary; 5 = Extremely necessary.
C = Cubans; D = Dominicans; PR = Puerto Ricans
SMC = Spanish for membership in the (ethnic) community; SMHLC = Spanish for membership in the Hispanic/Latino community
AG = Age group: 1 = 20–35; 2 = 36–50; 3 = 51 and over
TG = Total group

ranging from 1 = Not necessary at all to 5 = Extremely necessary. Their responses were averaged out.

These results show that first-generation Cubans and Dominicans feel that Spanish is between "very necessary" and "extremely necessary" for membership in their respective ethnic communities. They averaged 4.8 and 4.7 points, respectively. Puerto Ricans think it is between "necessary" and "very necessary," with 3.2 points. Cubans and Dominicans also feel that Spanish is between "very necessary" and "extremely necessary" for membership in the Hispanic/Latino community, with averages of 4.6 and 4.3, respectively. Puerto Ricans feel that Spanish is "very necessary" (4 points).

Among the second-generation members, Cubans and Dominicans think the same about Spanish for membership in their ethnic communities (averages of 4.1 and 4.5). Puerto Ricans also think the same, with 3.7 points. Cubans came ahead when it came to Spanish for membership in the Hispanic/Latino community as well, with 4.3 points. Puerto Ricans averaged

4.2 points, thus, these two groups think that Spanish is between "very neces-sary" and "extremely necessary." Dominicans think that Spanish is between "necessary" and "very necessary" (3.6 points).

The differences between generation and the importance subjects attrib-ute to Spanish as a requirement for membership in their ethnic community (p < .7388) and the Hispanic/Latino community (p < .3044) were not signif-icant. For first-generation subjects, Spanish is between "very necessary" and "extremely necessary" for membership in both communities, whereas for second-generation subjects it is between "very necessary" and "extremely necessary" for membership in their ethnic community, and "very necessary" for membership in the Hispanic/Latino community. Therefore, both groups recognize the role of the mother tongue when participating in the communi-ties they belong to for ethnic reasons. This language loyalty does not change, regardless of place of birth.

When it comes to gender, females perceive Spanish as a slightly more important requirement for membership in their ethnic communities than males. This difference proved to be insignificant (p < .2003). That was the case for membership in the Hispanic/Latino community, but this time, the difference was statistically significant (p < .0475).

Generation and ethnic group, and generation and gender were not pre-dictors of significant differences in this analysis.

Self-Evaluations of Four Major Skills in Spanish and English

The results for the self-evaluations of the four language skills done by the subjects are presented in four separate tables. The numbers refer to the av-erage in a scale in which 1 = Cannot read/write/speak/comprehend at all and 5 = Can read/write/speak/comprehend perfectly.

Table 4.14 includes the results of the reading skills. First-generation Cubans, Dominicans and Puerto Ricans evaluated their Spanish reading skills between "good" and "excellent."[4] Among this generation's members, Cubans and Puerto Ricans evaluated their English reading skills with an av-erage of 5 ("excellent"). Dominicans evaluated theirs between "good" and "excellent," with 4.8.

Cubans and Puerto Ricans from the second generation evaluated their Spanish reading skills between "average" and "good," whereas Dominicans evaluated theirs as "good." Cubans evaluated their English reading skills as "excellent." Dominicans and Puerto Ricans averaged be-tween "good" and "excellent."

First-generation Cubans, Dominicans, and Puerto Ricans evaluated their Spanish reading skills between "good" and "excellent." Among this

Table 4.14 Comparison of first- and second-generation Cubans, Dominicans, and Puerto Ricans based on their self-evaluation of their reading skills in Spanish and English

								Difference		
Generation		First			Second					
Ethnic group		C	D	PR	C	D	PR	C	D	PR
		SR*			SR*			SR*		
AG	1	4.8	4.7	5.0	3.5	4.3	3.3	-1.3	-0.4	-1.7
	2	5.0	4.8	4.5	4.3	4.0	3.0	-0.7	-0.8	-1.5
	3	5.0	5.0	5.0	3.0	3.7	3.0	-2.0	-1.3	-2.0
TG		4.9	4.8	4.8	3.8	4.0	3.1	-1.1	-0.8	-1.7
		ER*			ER*			ER*		
AG	1	4.3	2.3	4.7	5.0	5.0	5.0	+0.7	+2.7	+0.3
	2	3.8	2.9	4.3	5.0	5.0	4.2	+1.2	+2.1	-0.1
	3	3.5	2.3	3.7	5.0	4.3	5.0	+1.5	+2.0	+1.3
TG		3.9	2.6	4.2	5.0	4.8	4.6	+1.1	+2.2	+0.4

* Results are given in averages of points in the following scale: 1 = Cannot read at all; 2 = Poor reading skills; 3 = Average reading skills; 4 = Good reading skills; 5 = Can read perfectly.
C = Cubans; D = Dominicans; PR = Puerto Ricans
SR = Spanish reading skills; ER = English reading skills
AG = Age group: 1 = 20–35; 2 = 36–50; 3 = 51 and over
TG = Total group

generation's members, Cubans and Puerto Ricans evaluated their English reading skills with an average of 5 ("excellent"). Dominicans evaluated theirs between "good" and "excellent," with 4.8.

Cubans and Puerto Ricans from the second generation evaluated their Spanish reading skills between "average" and "good," whereas Dominicans evaluated theirs as "good." Cubans evaluated their English reading skills as "excellent." Dominicans and Puerto Ricans averaged between "good" and "excellent."

The second-generation members, regardless of ethnic group, evaluated their Spanish reading skills lower than their first-generation counterparts. The opposite happened on their evaluation of their English reading skills. Second-generation Puerto Ricans from age group 2 did not conform to this tendency.

Table 4.15 contains the results of the writing skills self-evaluations.

Generally speaking, Cubans, Dominicans, and Puerto Ricans from the first generation evaluated their Spanish writing skills between "good" and "excellent." Cubans and Puerto Ricans from this group evaluated their English writing skills between "average" and "good," whereas Dominicans from this group evaluated theirs between "poor" and "average."

Second-generation Dominicans evaluated their Spanish writing skills between "average" and "good," Cubans evaluated theirs as "average," and Puerto Ricans evaluated theirs between "poor" and "average." Cubans, on the other hand, evaluated their writing skills in English as "excellent." Dominicans and Puerto Ricans evaluated theirs between "good" and "excellent."

Comparing the first generation with the second generation, we can say that the second generation consistently evaluated their writing skills in Spanish lower than the first generation and that the first generation evaluated their English writing skills lower than the second generation. The group of Puerto Ricans from age group 2 is the exception.

Table 4.15 Comparison of first- and second-generation Cubans, Dominicans, and Puerto Ricans based on their self-evaluation of their writing skills in Spanish and English

								Difference		
Generation		First			Second					
Ethnic group		C	D	PR	C	D	PR	C	D	PR
		SW*			SW*			SW*		
AG	1	4.8	4.7	4.7	3.0	4.0	3.0	-1.8	-0.7	-1.7
	2	4.8	4.5	4.5	3.3	3.8	2.8	-1.5	-0.7	-1.7
	3	5.0	5.0	5.0	2.0	2.7	2.5	-3.0	-2.3	-2.5
TG		4.8	4.7	4.7	3.0	3.5	2.8	-1.8	-1.2	-1.9
		EW*			EW*			EW*		
AG	1	4.3	2.3	3.7	5.0	5.0	5.0	+0.7	+2.7	+1.3
	2	3.5	2.9	4.0	5.0	5.0	4.0	+1.5	+2.1	0.0
	3	1.5	2.0	2.7	5.0	4.3	5.0	+3.5	+2.3	+2.3
TG		3.4	2.5	3.5	5.0	4.8	4.5	+1.6	+2.3	+1.0

* Results are given in averages of points in the following scale:
1 = Cannot write at all; 2 = Poor writing skills; 3 = Average writing skills; 4 = Good writing skills; 5 = Can write perfectly.
C = Cubans; D = Dominicans; PR = Puerto Ricans
SW = Spanish writing skills; EW = English writing skills
AG = Age group: 1 = 20–35; 2 = 36–50; 3 = 51 and over
TG = Total group

Table 4.16 Comparison of first- and second-generation Cubans, Dominicans, and Puerto Ricans based on their self-evaluation of their speaking skills in Spanish and English

		First			Second			Difference		
Generation										
Ethnic group		C	D	PR	C	D	PR	C	D	PR
		SS*			SS*			SS*		
AG	1	5.0	5.0	5.0	4.3	5.0	4.0	-0.7	0.0	-1.0
	2	5.0	4.8	5.0	5.0	5.0	3.8	0.0	+0.2	-1.2
	3	5.0	5.0	5.0	3.0	4.7	3.5	-2.0	-0.3	-1.5
TG		5.0	4.9	5.0	4.4	4.9	3.8	-0.6	0.0	-1.2
		ES*			ES*			ES*		
AG	1	4.8	2.0	4.3	5.0	5.0	5.0	+0.2	+3.0	+0.7
	2	3.5	2.8	4.3	5.0	5.0	4.8	+1.5	+2.2	+0.5
	3	3.0	2.0	4.3	5.0	4.7	5.0	+2.0	+2.7	+0.7
TG		3.9	2.3	3.9	5.0	4.9	4.9	+1.1	+2.6	+1.0

* Results are given in averages of points in the following scale:
1 = Cannot speak at all; 2 = Poor speaking skills; 3 = Average speaking skills; 4 = Good speaking skills; 5 = Can speak perfectly.
C = Cubans; D = Dominicans; PR = Puerto Ricans
SS = Spanish speaking skills; ES = English speaking skills
AG = Age group: 1 = 20–35; 2 = 36–50; 3 = 51 and over
TG = Total group

The comparison of the speaking skills in Spanish and in English is included in Table 4.16. The first-generation groups with the highest evaluations of their Spanish speaking skills are the Cubans and Dominicans, with 5 points each ("excellent"). Puerto Ricans averaged 4.9. Cubans had the highest evaluations of their English speaking skills, with 3.9 points (between "average" and "good"), followed by the Puerto Rican subjects, with 3 points ("average"), and by the Dominican subjects, with 2.3 (between "poor" and "average").

The second-generation groups with the highest evaluations of their Spanish speaking skills are the Dominicans, with 4.9 points, and the Cubans, with 4.4 points (between "good" and "excellent"). The Puerto Rican subjects averaged 3.8 points (between "average" and "good"). Cubans had the highest evaluations of their English speaking skills, with 5 ("excellent"), followed by the Dominicans and Puerto Ricans, with 4.9 each.

The generalization we made before about the decrease in Spanish skills and increase in English skills among the second-generation subjects is true in this category as well. Dominicans from age group 2 are the exception this time.

Table 4.17 compares the listening comprehension skills of the subjects. All the first-generation subjects evaluated their listening comprehension skills in Spanish as "excellent" (5 points). Cubans and Puerto Ricans evaluated their skills in English between "good" and "excellent" (4.3 and 4.1 points, respectively). Dominicans evaluated theirs between "average" and "good."

Second-generation Dominicans evaluated their Spanish listening comprehension skills as "excellent" (5 points) whereas Cubans and Puerto Ricans evaluated theirs as "good" (4 points). All of them evaluated their skills in English as "excellent."

Table 4.17 Comparison of first- and second-generation Cubans, Dominicans, and Puerto Ricans based on their self-evaluation of their listening comprehension skills in Spanish and English

								Difference		
Generation		First			Second					
Ethnic group		C	D	PR	C	D	PR	C	D	PR
		SLC*			SLC*			SLC*		
AG	1	5.0	5.0	5.0	4.8	5.0	4.3	-0.2	0.0	-0.7
	2	5.0	5.0	5.0	5.0	5.0	4.0	0.0	0.0	-1.0
	3	5.0	5.0	5.0	4.0	5.0	4.0	-1.0	0.0	-1.0
TG		5.0	5.0	5.0	4.8	5.0	4.1	-0.2	0.0	-0.9
		ELC*			ELC*			ELC*		
AG	1	4.8	4.0	4.7	5.0	5.0	5.0	+0.2	+1.0	+0.3
	2	4.3	2.9	4.3	5.0	5.0	5.0	+0.7	+2.1	+0.7
	3	3.5	2.3	3.3	5.0	5.0	5.0	+1.5	+2.7	+1.7
TG		4.3	3.1	4.1	5.0	5.0	5.0	+0.7	+1.9	+0.9

* Results are given in averages of points in the following scale:
1 = Cannot comprehend at all; 2 = Poor listening comprehension skills; 3 = Average listening comprehension skills; 4 = Good listening comprehension skills; 5 = Can comprehend perfectly.
C = Cubans; D = Dominicans; PR = Puerto Ricans
SLC = Spanish listening comprehension skills; ELC = English listening comprehension skills
AG = Age group: 1 = 20–35; 2 = 36–50; 3 = 51 and over
TG = Total group

Once again, the idea of the decrease in the Spanish skills and increase in English skills among second-generation subjects holds true in this category. The exception this time is the group of Dominicans from age group 2. There is no difference between the first generation and second generation in their self-evaluation of their Spanish listening comprehension skills.

Overall, the generational differences are less marked in the subjects' evaluation of their speaking and listening comprehension skills. Second-generation members evaluated these skills in Spanish between "good" and "excellent." First-generation members evaluated their English skills between "average" and "good." In fact, the point difference for Spanish speaking and listening comprehension skills between the first- and the second-generation members is less than one (.57 for speaking and .4 for listening comprehension). One possible explanation is that these skills do not require knowledge of more formal and standard ways of speaking, thus allowing subjects to use more spontaneous forms of speech which, given the context, will be part of the speech they have to "comprehend" in interactions with others. Furthermore, listening is a receptive skill and does not involve the tension that productive skills such as writing can bring.

As expected, the generational variable determined statistically significant differences in the subjects' self-evaluation of Spanish and English skills. All the differences were significant. That is, first-generation members evaluate their Spanish skills significantly higher than second-generation members. The opposite holds true as well. As one might expect, being born in the U.S. is an indicator of better English reading ($p < .0002$), writing ($p < .0001$), speaking ($p < .0001$), and listening comprehension skills ($p < .0001$), as well as an indicator of less developed Spanish reading ($p < .0001$), writing ($p < .0001$), speaking ($p < .0001$), and listening comprehension skills ($p < .0050$), compared to the first generation.

The only significant difference determined by gender was in the self-evaluation of English-language reading skills ($p < .0492$). In general, males consider them between "very good" and "excellent" whereas females consider them between "good" and "very good."

The means for Spanish-language speaking skills ($p < .0007$) and Spanish-language listening comprehension skills ($p < .0076$) fluctuate from between "good" and "very good" to "excellent." English-language reading skills ($p < .0334$) and English-language speaking skills ($p < .0158$), on the other hand, fluctuate from between "poor" and "good" to "excellent." These fluctuations proved to be statistically significant considering the interaction between generation and ethnic group. Generally speaking, Spanish skills are poorer and English skills are better among the second-generation members of each ethnic group. This generalization, however, does not hold true specifically for the Spanish-language speaking skills and the Spanish-language listening comprehension skills of Dominicans.

There were other statistically significant differences determined by the independent variables generation and gender, specifically in English-language reading skills ($p < .0097$). Although the results imply that English-language reading skills improve significantly among second-generation females and males, a comparison of the means of each of the four sub-groups indicates that this improvement is more evident among females (from 2.94 in the first generation to 4.86 in the second generation). Once again, females determine the significance of the differences obtained with generation and gender as the independent variables.

Self-Comparisons of the Subjects' Skills in Spanish and English with Those of Others

The results of the subjects' comparisons of their overall skills in Spanish and in English with those of the adults who lived with them when they turned 13 years old; their siblings, relatives, and close friends; the other members of their ethnic communities; and those of other Hispanics/Latinos in the New York City area, are presented in four different tables. The numerical values of a five-point scale in which 1 = Worse, 3 = Same, and 5 = Better were averaged out and are included in these tables. Table 4.18 presents the results of the comparisons with the skills of the adults who lived with them on their 13th birthday.

This table suggests that Dominicans from the first generation believe that their overall skills in Spanish are between "somewhat better" and "better" than those of the adults who lived with them on their 13th birthday, with 4.3 points. Cubans and Puerto Ricans believe that theirs are between the "same" and "somewhat better" than those of these adults, with 3.6 and 3.8 points, respectively. All these subjects believe that their overall skills in English are between "somewhat better" and "better."

Among the second generation, Cubans and Puerto Ricans averaged 3.5 for overall skills in Spanish, which suggests that they believe these skills are between the "same" and "somewhat better" than those of the adults who lived with them. Dominicans averaged 2.9 points (between "somewhat worse" and the "same"). Finally, in terms of their overall skills in English, Dominicans and Puerto Ricans averaged 5 points ("better"), while Cubans averaged 4.8 points (between "somewhat better" and "better").

The results of the comparisons with the skills of their siblings, relatives, and close friends are included in Table 4.19.

Table 4.18 Comparison of first- and second-generation Cubans, Dominicans, and Puerto Ricans based on their self-comparison of their skills in Spanish and English with those of the adults who lived with them on their 13th birthday

								Difference		
Generation		First			Second					
Ethnic group		C	D	PR	C	D	PR	C	D	PR
		SA13*			SA13*			SA13*		
AG	1	2.8	4.3	4.0	3.8	3.7	3.3	+1.0	-0.6	-0.7
	2	4.3	4.5	3.5	2.7	2.5	3.6	-1.6	-2.0	+0.1
	3	4.0	3.8	4.0	5.0	2.7	3.5	+1.0	-1.1	-0.5
TG		3.6	4.3	3.8	3.5	2.9	3.5	-0.1	-1.4	-0.3
		EA13*			EA13*			EA13*		
AG	1	4.8	4.0	4.0	5.0	5.0	5.0	+0.2	+1.0	+1.0
	2	4.8	4.3	4.3	4.3	5.0	5.0	-0.5	+0.7	+0.7
	3	3.5	4.0	4.7	5.0	5.0	5.0	+1.5	+1.0	+0.3
TG		4.5	4.1	4.3	4.8	5.0	5.0	+0.3	+0.9	+0.7

* Results are given in averages of points in the following scale:
1 = Worse; 2 = Somewhat worse; 3 = Same; 4 = Somewhat better; 5 = Better.
C = Cubans; D = Dominicans; PR = Puerto Ricans
SA13 = Spanish skills compared to those of the adults who lived at home on the 13th birthday; EA13 = English skills compared to those of the adults who lived at home on 13th birthday
AG = Age group: 1 = 20–35; 2 = 36–50; 3 = 51 and over
TG = Total group

When the first-generation subjects compared their overall skills to those of their siblings, relatives, and close friends, Puerto Ricans averaged 4.1 points (between "somewhat better" and "better"), Cubans averaged 3.6 points and Dominicans averaged 3.8 points (both between the "same" and "somewhat better"). Cubans and Puerto Ricans averaged 3.7 (between the "same" and "somewhat better") when they compared their English skills to those of this group of people. Dominicans averaged 3 points (the "same").

All second-generation subjects evaluated their overall Spanish and English skills between "somewhat better" and "better" than those of their siblings, relatives, and close friends.

Table 4.20 presents the results of the comparisons with the skills of other members of the same ethnic community.

Table 4.19 Comparison of first- and second-generation Cubans, Dominicans, and Puerto Ricans based on their self-comparison of their skills in Spanish and English with those of their siblings, relatives, and close friends

								Difference		
Generation		First			Second					
Ethnic group		C	D	PR	C	D	PR	C	D	PR
		SSRF*			SSRF*			SSRF*		
AG	1	4.5	3.0	4.0	5.0	4.7	4.0	+0.5	+1.7	0.0
	2	3.5	4.5	4.0	3.7	3.8	3.4	+0.2	- 0.7	-0.6
	3	3.0	3.3	4.3	5.0	4.0	4.0	+2.0	+0.7	-0.3
TG		3.8	3.7	4.1	4.5	4.1	3.7	+0.7	+0.4	-0.4
		ESRF*			ESRF*			ESRF*		
AG	1	4.0	2.0	4.0	4.3	4.3	4.0	+0.3	+2.3	0.0
	2	4.0	4.3	4.0	4.3	3.8	4.2	+0.3	-0.5	+0.2
	3	2.5	2.3	3.0	4.0	4.3	4.0	+1.5	+2.0	+1.0
TG		3.7	3.0	3.7	4.3	4.1	4.1	+0.6	+ 1.1	+0.4

* Results are given in averages of points in the following scale:
1 = Worse; 2 = Somewhat worse; 3 = Same; 4 = Somewhat better; 5 = Better.
C = Cubans; D = Dominicans; PR = Puerto Ricans
SSRF = Spanish skills compared to those of their siblings, relatives, and close friends;
ESRF = English skills compared to those of their siblings, relatives, and close friends
AG = Age group: 1 = 20–35; 2 = 36–50; 3 = 51 and over
TG = Total group

Among the first-generation subjects, Puerto Ricans claimed that their overall skills in Spanish are between "somewhat better" and "better" than those of other Puerto Ricans (4.1 points). Cubans claimed that there are "somewhat better" (4 points) than those of other Cubans, while Dominicans claimed that theirs are between the "same" and "somewhat better" than those of other Dominicans. In terms of their overall skills in English, Cubans and Puerto Ricans claimed that theirs are between the "same" and "somewhat better" than those of other members of their communities (3.9 points and 3.3 points, respectively). Dominicans claimed that their skills are between "somewhat worse" and the "same," compared to those of other Dominicans.

All the second-generation subjects, regardless of ethnic group, evaluated their overall Spanish skills between the "same" and "somewhat better"

Table 4.20 Comparison of first- and second-generation Cubans, Dominicans, and Puerto Ricans based on their self-comparison of their skills in Spanish and English with those of the other members of the same ethnic community

								Difference		
Generation		First			Second					
Ethnic group		C	D	PR	C	D	PR	C	D	PR
		SC*			SC*			SC*		
AG	1	3.5	3.7	4.3	3.5	4.3	3.0	0.0	+0.6	- 1.3
	2	3.3	4.5	4.0	3.3	3.5	3.4	0.0	-1.0	-0.6
	3	4.5	3.7	4.0	3.0	3.0	3.0	-1.5	-0.7	-1.0
TG		3.6	4.0	4.1	3.4	3.6	3.2	-0.2	-0.4	-0.9
		EC*			EC*			EC*		
AG	1	4.8	3.0	3.7	5.0	4.7	4.0	+0.2	+1.7	+0.3
	2	3.0	3.5	3.8	4.7	4.3	4.8	+1.7	+0.8	+1.0
	3	4.0	2.0	2.3	5.0	4.7	4.0	+1.0	+2.7	+1.7
TG		3.9	2.9	3.3	4.9	4.5	4.4	+1.0	+2.0	+1.1

* Results are given in averages of points in the following scale:
1 = Worse; 2 = Somewhat worse; 3 = Same; 4 = Somewhat better; 5 = Better.
C = Cubans; D = Dominicans; PR = Puerto Ricans
SC = Spanish skills compared to those of the other members of the same ethnic community; EC = English skills compared to those of the other members of the same ethnic community
AG = Age group: 1 = 20–35; 2 = 36–50; 3 = 51 and over
TG = Total group

than those of the other members of their ethnic communities. The evaluation of their overall English skills is between "somewhat better" and "better."

The results of the comparisons with the skills of the members of the Hispanic/Latino community in general are in table 4.21. First-generation Cubans and Puerto Ricans claim that their overall skills in Spanish are between "somewhat better" and "better" than those of the other members of the Hispanic/Latino community (4.6 and 4.2 points, respectively). Dominicans claim that their skills are "somewhat better" (4 points). Puerto Ricans claim that their overall skills in English are "somewhat better" (4 points), Cubans claim that theirs are between the "same" and "somewhat better" (3.5 points), and Dominicans claim that they are between "somewhat worse" and the "same" (2.5 points).

Table 4.21 Comparison of first- and second-generation Cubans, Dominicans, and Puerto Ricans based on their self-comparison of their skills in Spanish and English with those of the members of the Hispanic/Latino community

							Difference		
Generation		First			Second				
Ethnic group	C	D	PR	C	D	PR	C	D	PR
		SC*			SC*			SC*	
		SHL*			SHL*			SHL*	
AG 1	4.8	4.0	4.3	4.3	4.3	3.3	-0.5	+0.3	-1.0
2	4.8	4.0	4.0	4.3	3.8	2.8	-0.5	-0.2	-1.2
3	4.0	3.7	4.3	3.0	3.3	3.0	-1.0	-0.4	-1.3
TG	4.6	4.0	4.2	4.1	3.9	3.0	-0.5	-0.1	-1.2
		EHL*			EHL*			EHL*	
AG 1	4.0	2.3	4.3	4.5	4.0	4.3	+0.5	+1.7	0.0
2	3.5	3.1	4.3	5.0	4.3	4.8	+1.5	+1.2	+0.5
3	2.5	1.7	3.3	5.0	4.0	5.0	+2.5	+2.3	+1.7
TG	3.5	2.5	4.0	4.8	4.1	4.7	+1.3	+1.6	+4.7

* Results are given in averages of points in the following scale:
1 = Worse; 2 = Somewhat worse; 3 = Same; 4 = Somewhat better; 5 = Better.
C = Cubans; D = Dominicans; PR = Puerto Ricans
SHL = Spanish skills compared to those of the members of the Hispanic/Latino community; EHL = English skills compared to those of the other members of the Hispanic/Latino community
AG = Age group: 1 = 20–35; 2 = 36–50; 3 = 51 and over
TG = Total group

Second-generation Cubans, on the other hand, claim that their overall skills are between "somewhat better" and "better" (4.1 points) than those of other Hispanics/Latinos, Dominicans claim that theirs are between the "same" and "somewhat better" (3.9 points), and finally, Puerto Ricans claim that theirs are the "same" (3 points). All the second-generation subjects believe that their overall skills in English are between "somewhat better" and "better." Cubans averaged 4.8 points, Dominicans 4.1 points, and Puerto Ricans 4.7 points.

In general, all the groups, regardless of generation and ethnic group, believe that their overall Spanish and English skills and the skills of others are not alike. In almost all the cases, the subjects evaluated their skills with an average above 3, meaning that they see their skills, generally, as "somewhat better" or "better." This also applies to second-generation subjects and their perceptions of their Spanish skills. The only exceptions are the first-generation Dominicans in their comparison of their overall English skills with those of the other members of their ethnic community and the members of the Hispanic/Latino community, as well as the second-generation Dominicans in their comparison of their overall Spanish skills with those of the adults who lived with them on their 13th birthday. In these three cases, the averages were below 3 points on the scale, meaning that they perceived their skills between "somewhat worse" and the "same." Finally, and generally speaking, the second-generation subjects showed a decrease in their evaluation of their Spanish skills compared to the first-generation subjects, and an increase in their evaluation of their English skills. As in the case of the self-evaluation of the four skills in Spanish and English, there are a few exceptions.

Domains

This section presents the results of the five questions that dealt with domains. These results are summarized in Table 4.22. The numbers included in this table correspond to the alternatives provided in the questionnaire after numerical values were assigned accordingly. Subjects had to indicate the language(s) by selecting one of these alternatives: A = Spanish only, B = Mostly Spanish, C = Both Spanish and English, D = Mostly English, and E = English only.

In the job environment, first-generation Dominicans and Cubans averaged between "mostly Spanish," and "both Spanish and English," with 2.3 and 2.7 points, respectively. Puerto Ricans averaged 3 points ("both Spanish and English"). There is more variation among the second-generation subjects. Puerto Ricans averaged between "mostly Spanish," and "both Spanish and English" (2.8 points), Dominicans averaged between "both Spanish and English," and "mostly English" (3.5 points), and Cubans averaged between "mostly English" and "English only" (4.5 points).

The order of the ethnic groups is practically inverted from one generation to the other. The low regard that Spanish had as a vehicle for economic progress for first-generation Puerto Ricans—compared to that indicated by Cubans and Dominicans—can be explained by the fact that this group, more than Cubans and Dominicans, uses more English in the job environment. It is interesting, however, that second-generation Puerto Ricans also regarded Spanish lower than the other groups in this category, and they use more Spanish on their jobs than the other groups.

When speaking with family members, Dominicans and Cubans averaged between "Spanish only" and "mostly Spanish" (1.7 points and 1.8

Table 4.22 Comparison of first- and second-generation Cubans, Dominicans, and Puerto Ricans based on the language(s) used in five domains

Generation			First			Second			Difference		
Ethnic group		C	D	PR	C	D	PR	C	D	PR
			J*			J*			J*		
AG	1	3.3	2.5	3.0	4.5	3.3	3.0	+1.2	+0.8	0.0
	2	3.0	2.5	2.8	4.3	3.3	3.0	+1.3	+0.8	+0.2
	3	2.0	2.0	2.3	5.0	4.0	2.5	+3.0	+2.0	+0.2
TG		3.0	2.3	2.7	4.5	3.5	2.8	+1.5	+1.2	+0.1
			FM*			FM*			FM*		
AG	1	2.0	1.3	2.0	2.0	2.0	3.0	0.0	+0.7	+1.0
	2	1.8	2.0	2.5	3.3	2.8	3.0	+1.5	+0.8	+0.5
	3	1.5	1.3	1.7	5.0	3.0	4.0	+3.5	+1.7	+2.3
TG		1.8	1.7	2.1	2.9	2.6	3.2	+1.1	+0.9	+1.1
			CF*			CF*			CF*		
AG	1	3.5	2.0	2.7	4.0	3.0	3.3	+0.5	+1.0	+0.6
	2	1.8	2.8	3.0	3.7	3.5	3.2	+1.9	+0.7	+0.2
	3	1.0	1.3	1.7	4.0	3.7	4.0	+3.0	+2.4	+2.3
TG		2.3	2.1	2.5	3.9	3.4	3.4	+1.6	+1.3	+0.9
			EC*			EC*			EC*		
AG	1	2.0	1.7	3.0	3.0	2.0	3.3	+1.0	+0.3	+0.3
	2	1.3	1.8	2.5	2.3	2.8	2.6	+1.0	+1.0	+0.1
	3	1.0	1.0	1.7	3.0	2.0	3.0	+2.0	+1.0	+1.3
TG		1.5	1.5	2.4	2.8	2.3	2.9	+1.3	+0.8	+0.5
			HL*			HL*			HL*		
AG	1	1.8	2.0	2.3	1.8	3.3	2.7	0.0	+1.3	+0.4
	2	1.8	2.0	2.5	2.7	2.8	2.4	+0.9	+0.8	-0.1
	3	1.5	1.3	1.7	3.0	1.7	2.5	+1.5	+0.4	+0.8
TG		1.7	1.8	2.2	2.3	2.6	2.5	+0.6	+0.8	+0.3

* Results are given in averages of points in the following scale:
1 = Spanish only; 2 = Mostly Spanish; 3 = Both Spanish and English; 4 = Mostly English; 5 = English only.
C = Cubans; D = Dominicans; PR = Puerto Ricans
J = Language(s) used on the job; FM = Language(s) used with family members;
CF = Language(s) used with close friends; C = Language(s) used with other members of the same ethnic community; HL = Language(s) used with other Hispanics/Latinos
AG = Age group: 1 = 20–35; 2 = 36–50; 3 = 51 and over
TG = Total group

points, respectively). Puerto Ricans averaged between "mostly Spanish," and "both Spanish and English," with 2.1 points. Second-generation Dominicans and Cubans averaged between "mostly Spanish," and "both Spanish and English" (2.6 and 2.9, respectively), while Puerto Ricans averaged between "both Spanish and English," and "mostly English" (3.2 points).

All the first-generation members prefer to use between "mostly Spanish," and "both Spanish and English" to speak with close friends (Dominicans 2.1 points, Cubans 2.3 points, and Puerto Ricans 2.5 points). Dominicans, Puerto Ricans, and Cubans from the second generation prefer between "both Spanish and English," and "mostly English" in this context (Dominicans and Puerto Ricans 3.4 points each, and Cubans 3.9 points).

In the context of speaking with other members of the same ethnic community, Cubans and Dominicans prefer between "Spanish only" and "mostly Spanish" (1.5 points each), whereas Puerto Ricans prefer between "mostly Spanish," and "both Spanish and English." All second-generation members also prefer to use between "mostly Spanish," and "both Spanish and English" (Dominicans 2.3 points, Cubans 2.8 points, and Puerto Ricans 2.9 points).

Finally, when speaking to other Hispanics/Latinos, Cubans and Dominicans prefer between "Spanish only" and "mostly Spanish" (1.7 points and 1.8 points, respectively), while Puerto Ricans prefer between "mostly Spanish," and "both Spanish and English" (2.2 points). This is also the preference of all the second-generation subjects, Cubans with 2.3 points, Puerto Ricans with 2.5 points, and Dominicans with 2.6 points.

The statistical analysis with generation as the independent variable shows that second-generation subjects use more English in all of the five domains, and that the difference between them and the first-generation subjects is significant (job: $p < .0007$, with family members: $p < .0001$, with close friends: $p < .0001$, with other members of the same ethnic community: $p < .0002$, and with other Hispanics/Latinos: $p < .0264$). In other words, being born in this country predicts a departure from the exclusive or almost exclusive use of Spanish in these domains. The least surprising results are those regarding language used in the job environment, given that first-generation members use between "mostly Spanish" and "both Spanish and English."

Although gender, and generation and gender did not yield any significant differences in the languages used in the five domains, generation and ethnic group determined significant differences in the language used in the job environment. The means vary from 2.3 (between "mostly Spanish" and "both Spanish and English") to 4.5 (between "mostly English" and "only English"). These results allow us to say that the use of English on the job increases significantly among the second-generation members of each ethnic group.

In the next section we present a brief summary of the findings discussed in detail in the previous section.

SUMMARY

Based exclusively on the data collected for this study, we established that there are no major differences in terms of place of birth, birth of the mother and the father, family constitution at age 13, and educational level attained among the three ethnic groups in each generation, and in some cases, even among generations. We also stated that Spanish is not the primary language of the home—that the second generation is using more English in this environment, and that first-generation individuals are making the switch as well. In addition, we described how Spanish competes with English in exposure to means of communication and usage in specific domains. Moreover, we emphasized the importance seen in the Spanish language for economic progress and membership in the ethnic and Hispanic/Latino community, and suggested that this is reinforced by the fact that, in general, individuals have solid and functional skills in the language, as well as a good perception of these skills when they compare them to those of others.

The analyses of variance proved that there are significant differences among first-generation and second-generation Cubans, Dominicans, and Puerto Ricans when generation, gender, generation and ethnic group, and generation and gender are taken into consideration. The generational factor accounted for more differences than any other independent variable(s), with seventeen out of the twenty-three dependent variables. Gender, and generation and ethnic group accounted for four, while generation and gender accounted for only two. This shows that the generation of which the individual is a member is the deciding element in most of the differences between first-generation and second-generation Cubans, Dominicans, and Puerto Ricans in New York City. Each generation behaves as a social and linguistic unity. Ethnicity and generation, gender and generation, and gender, on the other hand, do not predict such a behavior.

In chapter five we will discuss the results of the interview analysis, particularly, the retention of the allophones.

Results: Retention of Dialectal Phonetic Features among First- and Second-Generation Speakers of Cuban, Dominican, and Puerto Rican Spanish in the New York City Area

This chapter addresses the second issue explored in this study, that of the retention or non-retention of dialectal phonetic features in the speech of first-generation and second-generation Cubans, Dominicans, and Puerto Ricans in the New York City area. Fragments of the informants' speech samples were orthographically transcribed, phonetic contexts were identified, and retention of the selected phonemes was carefully determined. Retention indicates that the phoneme was realized as the standard allophone and did not suffer the neutralization processes that characterize the speech of the typical speaker of the given dialect of Spanish.

SUMMARY OF RESULTS

This section is divided into four parts: one part dedicated to each of the three ethnic groups and dialects followed by a final section with general observations about generational differences. Thus, the first section presents the results of the analysis of the speech of the Cuban subjects while the next two sections focus on the speech of the Dominican and Puerto Rican subjects, respectively. The discussion about generational differences is found in the last section.

Generational Differences in Cuban Spanish

The phonetic phenomena considered for this group, selected from the description of Cuban Spanish presented in Lipski (1994), were devoicing of /rr/, neutralization of /-r/, and neutralization of /-s/.

Devoicing of /rr/

The results are presented in Table 5.1. The first thing to point out is the fact that, contrary to what is stated by Lipski, /rr/ is not devoiced frequently enough to characterize it as a feature of Cuban Spanish. In fact, only first-generation members from age groups 1 and 2 devoiced it, 3 percent of the time the first group and 4 percent of the time the second one. None of the first-generation members from age group 3, and none of the second-generation members showed /rr/ devoicing in their speech.

Given this, differences in /rr/ devoicing are only evident in age groups 1 and 2, with second-generation members retaining the voiced feature of this phoneme 3 percent and 4 percent more, respectively. The second generation as a whole retains it 3 percent more than the first generation.

Perhaps it is necessary to say that this feature has lost its dialect-defining qualities among the first-generation group. Moreover, it does not seem to be salient enough for second-generation members to incorporate it as part of their speech.

Neutralization of /-r/

Table 5.2 presents the results. This table demonstrates that there is considerable variation among age groups. For instance, second-generation members from age groups 1 and 3 showed less retention of /-r/ in their speech (8

Table 5.1 Generational differences in /rr/ devoicing among speakers of Cuban Spanish

Age group	1		2		3		Total group	
Standard realizations*	$n\%$**		$n\%$**		$n\%$**		$n\%$**	
Generation								
First	29/30	97	35/37	96	19/19	100	83/86	97
Second	33/33	100	22/22	100	8/8	100	63/63	100
Percentage difference	+3		+4		0		+3	

* Results indicate number and percentage of phonetic contexts in which the phoneme *was not* realized as (one of) the expected allophone(s).
** Percentages are rounded out.

Table 5.2 Generational differences in /-r/ neutralization among speakers of Cuban Spanish

Age group	1	2	3	Total group
Standard realizations*	*n*%**	*n*%**	*n*%**	*n*%**
Generation				
First	50/167 30	36/134 27	14/34 19	100/375 27
Second	30/136 22	48/113 42	2/32 6	80/281 28
Percentage difference	-8	+15	-13	+1

* Results indicate number and percentage of phonetic contexts in which the phoneme *was not* realized as (one of) the expected allophone(s).
** Percentages are rounded out.

percent and 13 percent less, respectively). Second-generation members from age group 2, on the other hand, showed considerably more retention and less neutralization (15 percent). Considering all Cuban subjects, there are no differences. Second-generation Cubans retained /-r/ only 1 percent more than their first-generation counterparts.

Neutralization of /-s/

These results are presented in table 5.3. The only age group that showed considerable differences was group 3. Second-generation members from this age group neutralized /-s/ 8 percent less frequently than first-generation members. As a group, Cubans showed no major differences with regard to this feature. This behavior corresponds to that shown by all the subjects—from the three ethnic groups—combined.

Table 5.3 Generational differences in /-s/ neutralization among speakers of Cuban Spanish

Age group	1	2	3	Total group
Standard realizations*	*n*%**	*n*%**	*n*%**	*n*%**
Generation				
First	36/465 8	23/350 7	5/283 2	64/1,098 6
Second	35/400 9	14/349 4	7/70 10	56/819 7
Percentage difference	+1	-3	+8	+1

* Results indicate number and percentage of phonetic contexts in which the phoneme *was not* realized as (one of) the expected allophone(s).
** Percentages are rounded out.

Generational Differences in Dominican Spanish

To analyze the speech of the Dominican subjects we considered three phonetic phenomena selected from the description of Dominican Spanish presented by Lipski (1994). These phenomena were neutralization of /-r/, neutralization of /-s/, and neutralization of /-l/.

Neutralization of /-r/

The results are presented in Table 5.4. This table reveals that second-generation members from age groups 2 and 3 neutralize /-r/ considerably more than first-generation members (20 percent and 25 percent, respectively). Second-generation members from age group 1, however, show the opposite. They neutralize this phoneme with 10 percent less frequency. As a group, second-generation Dominicans show 13 percent less retention, a clear indication of what I suggested earlier about this phenomenon decreasing among the second generation (excluding Cubans).

Neutralization of /-s/

Table 5.5 presents the results. There are differences among the first generation and the second generation, but these differences are not as marked as those found in /-r/ retention. Generally speaking, age groups 1 and 3 retained slightly more frequently (4 percent and 3 percent more, respectively), and age group 2 retained slightly less frequently (6 percent less).

Neutralization of /-l/

Although /-l/ neutralization also occurs in Cuban and Puerto Rican Spanish, this phoneme was not taken into consideration with these two ethnic groups.

Table 5.4 Generational differences in /-r/neutralization among speakers of Dominican Spanish

Age group	1	2	3	Total group
Standard realizations*	n%**	n%**	n%**	n%**
Generation				
First	28/119 24	67/159 42	36/125 29	131/403 33
Second	45/134 34	36/162 22	5/124 4	86/420 20
Percentage difference	+10	-20	-25	-13

* Results indicate number and percentage of phonetic contexts in which the phoneme *was not* realized as (one of) the expected allophone(s).
** Percentages are rounded out.

Table 5.5 Generational differences in /-s/neutralization among speakers of Dominican Spanish

Age group	1	2	3	Total group
Standard realizations*	*n*%**	*n*%**	*n*%**	*n*%**
Generation				
First	18/306 6	58/429 14	41/377 11	131/1,112 11
Second	30/302 10	34/447 8	38/279 14	102/1,028 10
Percentage difference	+4	-6	+3	-1

* Results indicate number and percentage of phonetic contexts in which the phoneme *was not* realized as (one of) the expected allophone(s).
** Percentages are rounded out.

This decision was made, in part, because Dominican Spanish has more allophonic realizations for this particular phoneme than Cuban and Puerto Rican Spanish. The results for neutralization of /-l/ are presented in Table 5.6.

The results show that second-generation members from age groups 1 and 2 retained /-l/ less frequently than first-generation members from these groups (5 percent and 3 percent less, respectively). Members from age group 3, however, retained it 1 percent more. If we consider all Dominican subjects, second-generation members neutralized this phoneme with 3 percent more frequency than first-generation members. The differences do not appear to be significant. The most common forms of neutralization of /-l/ were vocalization and rotacism.

Table 5.6 Generational differences in /-l/neutralization among speakers of Dominican Spanish

Age group	1	2	3	Total group
Standard realizations*	*n*%**	*n*%**	*n*%**	*n*%**
Generation				
First	67/71 94	123/129 95	86/100 86	276/300 92
Second	101/114 89	100/109 92	68/78 87	269/301 89
Percentage difference	-5	-3	+1	-3

* Results indicate number and percentage of phonetic contexts in which the phoneme *was not* realized as (one of) the expected allophone(s).
** Percentages are rounded out.

Generational Differences in Puerto Rican Spanish

The features considered from this dialect were also selected from the description of Puerto Rican Spanish presented by Lipski (1994). These features were neutralization of /-r/, neutralization of /-s/, and velarization or uvularization of /rr/.

Neutralization of /-r/

The results are presented in table 5.7. In general, second-generation speakers of Puerto Rican Spanish neutralize /-r/ 12 percent more frequently than first-generation speakers of this dialect. Members of age groups 1 and 2 determined this increase, with 31 percent and 4 percent more frequency. Age group 3, however, showed a different linguistic behavior. Second-generation members from this group neutralized /-r/ 7 percent less frequently than their first-generation counterparts.

Neutralization of /-s/

Table 5.8 presents the results. The differences in retention of /-s/ among first-generation and second-generation Puerto Ricans are not significant. Second-generation members from age groups 1 and 3 retained it with 4 percent more frequency while those from age group 2 retained it with 2 percent less frequency. The whole second-generation group retained /-s/ with 2 percent more frequency.

Velarization or Uvularization of /rr/

These results are presented in table 5.9. These results reveal, first of all, that velarization or uvularization of /rr/ are not as common as it is widely thought. In fact, the use of velar or uvular /rr/ varies greatly among Puerto

Table 5.7 Generational differences in /-r/ neutralization among speakers of Puerto Rican Spanish

Age group	1	2	3	Total group
Standard realizations*	*n*%**	*n*%**	*n*%**	*n*%**
Generation				
First	70/159 44	32/140 23	21/93 23	123/392 31
Second	14/112 13	39/205 19	19/63 30	72/380 19
Percentage difference	-31	-4	+7	-12

* Results indicate number and percentage of phonetic contexts in which the phoneme *was not* realized as (one of) the expected allophone(s).
** Percentages are rounded out.

Table 5.8 Generational differences in /-s/ neutralization among speakers of Puerto Rican Spanish

Age group	1	2	3	Total group
Standard realizations*	*n*%**	*n*%**	*n*%**	*n*%**
Generation				
First	76/314 2	66/444 15	9/230 4	82/988 8
Second	21/341 6	71/555 13	16/210 8	108/1,106 10
Percentage difference	+4	-2	+4	+2

* Results indicate number and percentage of phonetic contexts in which the phoneme *was not* realized as (one of) the expected allophone(s).
** Percentages are rounded out.

Ricans living in the island. Only the group of first-generation members from age group 3 neutralized /rr/ at considerable rates (92 percent percent of the time). The other groups ranged from 29 percent of the time to 0 percent of the time. Second-generation members from age groups 2 and 3 retain the alveolar feature of /rr/ 1 percent and 92 percent more than first-generation members from these age groups. Only the youngest group of second-generation members retained it less, 23 percent. As a group, the retention among second-generation members is 21 percent more frequent.

Velarization and uvularization of /rr/ are highly stigmatized not only among speakers of other dialects of Spanish, but also among Puerto Ricans themselves. This stigmatization may be having an effect on the way speakers of Puerto Rican Spanish in the New York City area speak. The results

Table 5.9 Generational differences in /rr/ velarization or uvularization among speakers of Puerto Rican Spanish

Age group	1	2	3	Total group
Standard realizations*	*n*%**	*n*%**	*n*%**	*n*%**
Generation				
First	30/32 94	37/46 80	3/37 8	70/115 61
Second	20/28 71	65/80 81	23/23 100	108/131 82
Percentage difference	-23	+1	+92	+21

* Results indicate number and percentage of phonetic contexts in which the phoneme *was not* realized as (one of) the expected allophone(s).
** Percentages are rounded out.

reveal that this phenomenon is still prevalent among the oldest section of native-born Puerto Ricans and that there are great differences when we compare this group with the youngest native-born section. The latter group velarizes or uvularizes /rr/ with 86 percent less frequency than the former group. However, if one considers the second-generation group, there seems to be a return to velarization and uvularization of /rr/. The youngest section of this group retains /rr/ with 10 percent less frequency than those in age group 2, and with 29 percent less frequency than the oldest group. One possible explanation for this may be the idea that this type of neutralization of /rr/ may respond to affiliation and patriotic purposes, for some "have adopted it as the most 'Puerto Rican' of all sounds" (Lipski 1994, 334).

In the next section we will discuss some general findings based on the generational factor.

Generational Differences and the Neutralization of /-r/ and /-s/

The only two phonetic features shared by the three dialects—from those selected in this study—are neutralization of /-r/ and neutralization of /-s/. In this section we present and discuss the results for all the subjects included in the study only taking into consideration the generational issue.

Generally speaking, second-generation members retain /-r/ less frequently than first-generation members (8 percent less frequently). That is, /-r/ in the speech of second-generation members suffers neutralization at a higher rate than in the speech of first-generation members. This is more evident among members of age group 3, with 12 percent less, followed by age group 1, with 10 percent less, and age group 2, with 5 percent less.

These findings suggest that there is a slight generational difference in the neutralization of /-r/, a phonetic feature that is highly regarded as characteristic of the Caribbean dialects of Spanish. First-generation members neutralized it 70 percent of the time while second-generation members neutralized 78 percent of the time. Perhaps this is a clearly salient feature of the speech that second-generation speakers are exposed to, and is easily incorporated into their own speech, to the point that it is apparently manifested at higher rates. Based on the results discussed above, Cubans are the exception to this tendency; specifically, Cubans from age group 2 were responsible for this ethnic group not conforming to the overall trend. Dominicans and Puerto Ricans are the ones supporting this idea.

Despite this, the statistical analysis showed that generation, generation and gender, and generation and ethnic group do not determine significant differences when considered as independent variables. In fact, generation, as well as generation and ethnic group, did not yield any statistically significant differences for any of the phono-phonetic features considered in this study.

The results for neutralization of /-s/ vary among groups. Second-generation members from age groups 1 and 3 demonstrated more retention of /-s/ (2 percent more and 5 percent more, respectively) while members of age group 2 demonstrated less retention (3 percent less). Overall, percentage differences are minimal, and this applies to the entire group of subjects as well (1 percent more).

Neutralization of /-s/ is also known as a typical feature of Caribbean Spanish. This feature slightly decreased among second-generation members. This may sound surprising since /-s/ suffers neutralization more frequently than /-r/ (22 percent more frequently among first-generation members and 13 percent more frequently among second-generation members).

According to the statistical analysis, generation, and generation and ethnic group do not determine significant differences. Nevertheless, it is evident that generation and gender interact with the levels of /-s/ retention (p < .0266). Second-generation females retain it significantly more than first-generation females. The exact opposite occurs among males. Second-generation males retain /-s/ significantly less than their first-generation counterparts. Consider Figure 5.1.

SUMMARY

The summary of results demonstrated that there are no great differences in the speech of first-generation and second-generation Cubans, Dominicans, and Puerto Ricans in the New York City area. Percentages of phonetic feature retention do not vary considerably among subjects from these generation and ethnic groups. There are only two phonemes that point to generational differences: retention of /-r/ (primarily among speakers of Dominican and Puerto Rican Spanish), and retention of /rr/ among speakers

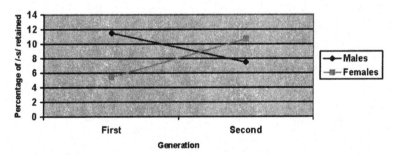

Figure 5.1 Distribution of means for generation and gender, and retention of /-s/

of Puerto Rican Spanish. The former appears to be decreasing among second-generation speakers and the latter appears to be increasing.

In this chapter we also approached the question of whether or not generational and ethnic factors interact with rates of retention of phono-phonetic features, and the answer provided by the statistical analysis appears to be that they do not—except for generation and gender, and retention of /-s/, where there is a clear interaction. Thus, speakers from both generations retain and neutralize at comparable rates. Having been born in the U.S. and being different from the first-generation members in many aspects does not mean that second-generation members have marked differences in their speech, as far as the studied phonemes is concerned.

In chapter six we will discuss the findings of this study in light of the theoretical framework provided by the literature on Spanish in the United States and provide some concluding remarks.

Chapter Six
Discussion and Conclusions

This study attempted to uncover established generational and dialectal differences among Cubans, Dominicans, and Puerto Ricans, living in the New York City area. In this chapter we will discuss the main differences—or absence of differences—uncovered. Particularly, we will dedicate part of the discussion to the generational issue and another part to the dialectal issue, for each one represents one of the goals of this investigation. Nevertheless, these issues will be pointed out and alluded to throughout the discussion because of their interrelated nature. Other important aspects of the study will permeate the discussion as well. We will comment on the limitations of the study, and on some projections and suggestions for future research. Finally, we will present some concluding remarks in light of the most relevant findings of the study.

ON GENERATIONS

The depiction of Spanish in the United States presented in the literature describes a somewhat questionable situation regarding its maintenance and vitality. This investigation supports, to an extent, that observation. The first aspect of the situation surrounding first-generation and second-generation Cubans, Dominicans, and Puerto Ricans in this geographical area is the language(s) they use in the home setting. Recent immigrants, evidently, grew up in a home were Spanish was widely or exclusively used for communication. Descendents of immigrants, on the other hand, also grew up in homes were Spanish was widely used, despite the unquestionable use of English. Both cohorts, nonetheless, live in homes where English is used more often than in the homes in which they grew up. A qualification is in place. First-generation members have already integrated the new linguistic code in the communication that takes place in this setting. If we compare the linguistic situation of the home settings in which members of the second generation grew up, many predictions can be established. The second generation of the future is being exposed to more English at home. If the pattern verified in the current second generation is that the use of English increases once they reach adulthood, then one can expect the second generation of the future to continue integrating even more English. The home has been considered the domain that guarantees language maintenance, even the cause of the relative success that Hispanics/Latinos have had (Hayden 1966). Unfortunately, this may change several generations from now.

The results regarding language(s) used at home confirmed what García et al. (1988) reported on Cubans, Dominicans, and Puerto Ricans in New York City. In this environment, Dominicans use more Spanish than Cubans and Puerto Ricans. First-generation and second-generation Dominicans reported more use of Spanish in the home at age 13 and at the present time.

New York City is a good place to live for those Hispanics/Latinos who want to stay connected to their mother tongue via means of communication. Here, radio and TV stations, music stores, and the press cater to the linguistic needs and preferences of this cohort. With more than four radio stations, two TV stations, and access to many musical genres and publications in Spanish, Hispanics/Latinos have many choices when it comes to media. These choices bring multiple results. Overall, the first generation prefers Spanish means of communication compared to the second generation, with a few exceptions. First, members of the first generation and second generation watch more English-language TV than Spanish-language TV. Younger Cubans do not conform to this generalization. (The differences between the first generation and second generation, nevertheless, were significant.) Second, although the first generation reads newspapers and magazines in Spanish with more frequency than in English, they evidently read more in English than what the second generation reads in Spanish. They have already accommodated what is available in English into their reading habits. (The difference in the frequency with which subjects read in Spanish was significant for generation. The difference in English was not.) First-generation Puerto Ricans are the exception; they read more in English than in Spanish.

Part of the relative force that Spanish has in the New York City area lies in how Hispanics/Latinos see this language, and the value they attribute to it. In general, first-generation and second-generation Cubans, Dominicans, and Puerto Ricans believe that Spanish—as well as English—is very important for economic progress. (There were no significant differences for generation.) Some of the subjects pointed out that the continuous flow of immigrants in the City calls for people who are dominant in Spanish, people who can provide services to Spanish monolinguals. The emphasis is placed on the capacity to communicate with this sector of the Hispanic community, not on whether jobs specifically require Spanish skills or not.

Interestingly, English is less important than Spanish for first-generation Cubans and second-generation Puerto Ricans. The first group has been able to have economic success—especially those living west of the Hudson River—without having to have absolute control of the English language. The second group's opinion represents an ironic point of view of these two languages. We have already mentioned that this group includes the descendants of the first wave of Puerto Ricans that came to this city over fifty years ago. These Puerto Ricans had to function in a society in which laws and privileges for immigrants were scarce. This group, more than any other group, should value the need of English skills for economic progress. Perhaps there are reasons of a psychological nature that determine their posture with regard to this topic.

Spanish is also valued for its identity power. It is seen as a ticket for membership into the ethnic community and the Hispanic/Latino community. Some level of Spanish proficiency is thus necessary to have a sense of belonging in these communities. There are, however, differences in terms of how necessary Spanish is. For instance, Puerto Ricans believe that Spanish is more necessary to belong in the Hispanic/Latino community than to belong in the Puerto Rican community. Dominicans have the opposite opinion. Cubans, on the other hand, show some generational differences. Spanish is more necessary to belong in the Cuban community, according to first-generation Cubans. Second-generation Cubans believe that it is more necessary to belong in the Hispanic/Latino community.

Zentella (1990c) provides contradictory arguments. She reports that the Puerto Rican students she interviewed had a clear sense of identity regardless of language choice. These youngsters also believed that it was possible to be Puerto Rican without knowing how to speak Spanish. Perhaps the age factor is a determinant. All of the people who participated in our study were over twenty years old. In fact, Zentella (1982) mentions the renewal of the Spanish skills of those adults who maintain contact with the community and with recent immigrants, and some of the informants mentioned that proficiency in Spanish is needed to be able to communicate with new immigrants. This may well be a process that will change the opinions of Zentella's young informants.

The discussion presented above provides some support to Fishman's (1966a) notion of ethnicity among the second generation. As we stated in chapter two, he argues that the second generation only maintains a positive attitude towards the ethnic culture and language. It is obvious that Cubans,

Dominicans, and Puerto Ricans born in this country do maintain a positive attitude toward Spanish and their culture in general; however, they have been able to maintain more than that. As we will discuss briefly, these individuals have acquired some control of the four major skills in Spanish. Therein may lie the success of Spanish over other minority languages. Furthermore, Fishman says that language maintenance is guaranteed when there is distance from what is considered American. Once again, second-generation Cubans, Dominicans, and Puerto Ricans in this area have not subscribed to this behavioral pattern. They report to have excellent skills in the English language, see its need for economic advancement, and use it in many linguistic domains.

The value that Cubans, Dominicans, and Puerto Ricans impose on Spanish for membership in the community is in tune with what Romaine (1995) points out, but in a different direction. She claims that support from the host community aids language maintenance, but in this case it is the immigrant community the one that is providing support to itself. This support takes the form of membership in the community, with all the psychologically- and identity-oriented benefits it brings. Membership is granted under the condition that proficiency in Spanish is exhibited, the linguistic pre-requisite is imposed, and some level of maintenance is achieved by those seeking membership. Furthermore, there is a cyclic relationship between functioning in the community and competency in the language. As Hofman (1971) points out when speaking about the Puerto Rican community, the more one functions within the value system of the community, the more one will be impelled to speak the linguistic variant required by that system.

We have discussed the value Cubans, Dominicans, and Puerto Ricans place on Spanish in New York City, and how that is manifested in the home setting. Let us consider the linguistic skills developed by these individuals. For the most part, the first generation claims to have better Spanish skills than English skills whereas the second generation claims to have better English skills than Spanish skills. (All the generational differences for the four skills in both languages were significant.) A few relevant facts merit consideration. First of all, and relying on their self-evaluations, members of the second generation have been able to develop solid reading, writing, speaking, and listening comprehension skills in Spanish. This applies to the three ethnic groups alike. They feel more comfortable, nonetheless, with their speaking and listening comprehension skills. This reflects the relationship that most second-generation members have had with Spanish: they grew up being exposed to it and using it in conversations, but they were not educated to be able to read it and write it, more formal expressions of language acquisition. Moreover, second-generation members report that their Spanish speaking and listening comprehension skills are better than what the first generation reports for their English speaking and listening comprehension skills. Compared to the first generation, the second generation has attained better control of these two skills in the language in which they feel less dominant. In fact, second-generation Dominicans rated their Spanish and English speaking skills the same. The situation appears to be promising, for as Stone (1987) implies, we will need to count on adults with proficiency in Spanish for this language to keep existing in the United States.

The comparisons that the subjects made of their linguistic skills and the linguistic skills of others reflect, generally speaking, that they perceive those skills to be between the "same" and "better," never "poorer"—particularly when the first-generation members compare their Spanish skills with those of others and when the second-generation members compare their English skills with those of others. This reflects the confidence that first-generation members have in their English skills and the confidence the second-generation members have in their Spanish skills. Both generations feel that their English skills are better than those of the adults who lived with them on their 13th birthday, except for the first-generation Dominicans. That includes the monolingual parents of the members of the first generation and the immigrant parents of the members of the second generation. There is considerable variation in the comparisons with the skills of other groups. For example, when comparing their skills with those of other members of the same ethnic community, first-generation Cubans and all the members of the second generation evaluated their English skills higher on the scale—between the "same" and "better"—than they evaluated their Spanish skills. First-generation Dominicans and Puerto Ricans did the opposite: their comparisons of the Spanish skills were higher for Spanish than they were for English. Finally, when comparing their skills with the skills of other Hispanics/Latinos, the first generation consistently evaluated their Spanish skills higher on the scale—once again, between "same" and "better"—than their English skills, and vice versa for the second generation.

One interesting issue raised by these results has to do with the Puerto Rican community. This ethnic group is more represented than the other two, and by a large margin. Second-generation Puerto Ricans, nevertheless, ranked below Cubans and Dominicans in their self-evaluations of their Spanish-language speaking and listening comprehension skills. Based on Y. R. Solé's (1987) claim that each group shows more Spanish maintenance where its members are the most represented, one would expect Puerto Ricans to have come on top, but that was not the case. This makes one wonder about the self-evaluations that Puerto Ricans living in other areas would make of their overall Spanish skills.

Another interesting issue raised by the results is the lack of confirmation of what Portes and Rumbaut (1996) state about Cubans. These authors argue that Cubans claim to be more fluent in English and in Spanish than the other groups. According to the result of the study being discussed here, first-generation Cubans share the highest average with Puerto Ricans for Spanish and English speaking skills. Second-generation Cubans are second to Dominicans for Spanish speaking skills. The only case in which Cubans had the highest average was in English speaking skills among the second-generation members.

It is important to note what the analysis for gender and self-evaluation of linguistic skills revealed, particularly, the evaluation of Spanish skills. Y. R. Solé (1990); Hidalgo (1993); and Portes and Schauffler (1994) claim that females retain the mother tongue more than males, but our analysis did not confirm this notion. In fact, women reported to have better reading skills in English than men did. The results did not confirm what Zentella (1982) argues about females in the Puerto Rican community of New York City either. She attributed more retention among females to their seclusion in the home environment. Based on the results alone, it would be impossible, nevertheless, to claim that the opposite is happening. We cannot state, as Klee (1987) says referring to Mexican-American females, that women shift more to English because they accept outgroup values more easily. More detailed research is needed to address these specific findings of this investigation.

The linguistic skills that the first generation has developed in English and that the second generation has developed in Spanish is reflected in the languages they use in different domains. This is important for, as Silva-Corvalán (1992) says, the more domains in which Spanish is used, the more competence its speakers will have in the language. Spanish is used—at various levels—in the job environment, with family members, with close friends, with other members of the same ethnic community, and with other Hispanics/Latinos; but English has clearly infiltrated the job environment and interactions with close friends, more so than the other three domains. The second generation steadily reported using more English than the first generation in the five domains. Among the members of the later group, Puerto Ricans reported higher values on the scale than did Cubans and Dominicans. It is hard to say for the second generation. Cubans and Puerto Ricans reported higher values on the scales for two domains, respectively, whereas Dominicans reported higher values than Cubans and Puerto Ricans in one domain.

The results revealed what García et al. (1988) argued: among Puerto Ricans and Cubans it is more common to use both Spanish and English with their parents, siblings, and children—family—than among Dominicans. On the contrary, the results do not suggest what Hidalgo discusses about Mexican-Americans in Chula Vista, California. In this community, the younger generation felt more strongly about English because of its role for personal and developmental purposes. Cubans, Dominicans, and Puerto Ricans in the New York City area not only see the value of Spanish, but also employ it in domains that relate to their personal and developmental needs. Another point of contrast regarding the perceived value of Spanish is that Hidalgo's older informants saw more value in Spanish than the younger generation for activities such as doing business and traveling. This does not seem to be the case among Cubans, Dominicans, and Puerto Ricans in New York City either.

In sum, this study reveals that English permeates certain circumstances and domains—like the home and job settings—but it has not affected other aspects surrounding Cubans, Dominicans, and Puerto Ricans in the New York City area. At a psychological level, Spanish is perceived as very important for economic and identity reasons. At a more practical level, Spanish co-exists with English in many domains and the second generation has been able to acquire sufficient skills to function with confidence in these domains as well as in their communities. The result is a mixture of negative and positive aspects. The commitment to Spanish and the linguistic skills are enough for Spanish to survive in the immediate future, with tremendous variations, though. On the other hand, Cubans, Dominicans, and Puerto Ricans seem to be behaving as a unity. In other words, both generations are responding to the immigration experience in similar fashions, each one as a "uniform" group—and despite the lack of evidence of language leveling. We can thus speak of inter-group tendencies and comportment, not intragroup.

ON DIALECTS

One of the purposes of the study was to determine whether or not there were differences in the speech of first-generation and second-generation speakers of the same dialect. The comparisons were based on three phonemes per ethnic group. These phonemes normally suffer some type of neutralization, and these neutralizations, together with others, characterize and distinguish these dialects from others. There were two phonemes that were considered for the three dialects. The third phoneme considered for each dialect was different.

The results of the analysis showed that there were no significant differences in the way first-generation and second-generation members of each ethnic group speak. The members of each generation realized the phonemes as the standard allophone—and as the neutralized allophone—with very similar frequencies. Second-generation speakers of each dialect thus speak a variant of Spanish that resembles that of their ancestors.

Despite these findings, some observations may be pointed out. Generally speaking, there was less retention of /-r/ among the second generation. No major differences were found with regard to /-s/, except when the generational factor was combined with the gender factor. Among Cubans, there were no relevant differences whatsoever. Among Dominicans, the second generation retained /-r/ less frequently. Finally, among Puerto Ricans, the second generation retained /-r/ less frequently and retained /rr/ more frequently.

All in all, this study proved that the acquisition of Spanish amid second-generation members allows them to speak a variety that does not differ enormously from that spoken by the first-generation members, at least as far as the realization of a specific group of phonemes is concerned. When these individuals speak, they are capable of integrating speech features that typify the dialect they speak. The parallel use of English and Spanish around them, and being in contact with speakers of other varieties of Spanish and other languages, do not alter the acquisition of particular pronunciation patterns. In the long run this acquisition is similar to the acquisition they would experience living in the motherland.

LIMITATIONS OF THE STUDY AND SUGGESTIONS FOR FUTURE RESEARCH

The study herein presented has several limitations that may and should be addressed in the future. First of all, the limited number of subjects utilized forced us to take precautions when making generalizations. A larger sample of individuals would strengthen the data set and would allow for more powerful conclusions. This limitation applies more directly on the second-generation Cubans cohort, especially those from age group 3—50 years old or over. We only included one subject in this category and avoided alluding to it as much as possible.

Another limitation has to do with the analyses performed and discussed in chapter four. It is necessary to explore the interactions between other factors and the variables encompassed in the five groupings mentioned in chapter three. We only considered generation, gender, generation and gender, and generation and ethnic group for a very important reason: the main focus of the investigation was the generational and dialectal differences among Cubans, Dominicans, and Puerto Ricans living in the New York City area, and considering other factors would have shifted or altered the focus. Thus, we propose further research on the situation of these three groups in this geographical region by evaluating issues such as the relationship between language of the home at age 13 and the self-evaluation of Spanish and English skills, and the effects of education and economic status on the perceived relevance of Spanish as a requirement for membership in the ethnic and Hispanic/Latino community.

The last limitation we will point out is that it is difficult to establish similarities and differences in the way first-generation and second-generation members of a particular ethnic group speak when only three phonemes are considered. Ideally, such endeavor would entail the evaluation of—at least—phonetic, syntactic, and lexical traits. Such a task was outside of the realm of this study; nevertheless, if the objective is to make more thorough comparisons, all these aspects of an individual's linguistic competence must be taken into consideration.

We would like to provide other suggestions for future research. First of all, a longitudinal study is needed to investigate the effects of exposure to English among the younger members of the first generation and to determine if the use of English in the home and job settings and in interactions with others increases over time. Moreover, a well-designed longitudinal investigation would provide more insights into the effects that the linguistic issues approached in this study have on one's sense of identity and ethnicity. Such studies would concentrate on the process of change—if there is any—rather than on the prevailing conditions at a particular moment in time. This would be tremendously beneficial for scholars interested in language planning and language change, and more importantly, it would be of great interest to those trying to combat the disappearance of Spanish in the United States.

Finally, in this study we used informants who belonged to the first generation or second generation of one of the ethnic groups already mentioned. These informants were related to others by family ties or friendship. Nonetheless, very few of them had a parent-child relationship. To consider this would allow for more direct connections between the first generation—the parents—and the second generation—the children—and for comparisons between the linguistic expectations the first generation had for their succeeding generation and the real outcome. Just as in our study, the sociolinguistic profile of each generation should be complemented with an analysis of their speech.

CONCLUDING REMARKS

The competition between the Spanish language and the dominant language in this country has had two main consequences. First, it has tested the endurance of both languages in those domains in which they have been used and are still used. Second, it has forced speakers of Spanish and their descendants—those with skills in the mother tongue—to make linguistic decisions. These decisions may be of an ideological or a performance nature, but regardless of their essence, these decisions reveal intergroup trends more than they reveal intragroup trends. Decisions of an ideological nature—e.g., role of Spanish in community membership—may be linked to ethnicity issues and do not vary dramatically across ethnic or generational boundaries. Decisions that actually involve performance and a specific linguistic competence, on the other hand, show that Cubans, Dominicans, and Puerto Ricans living in the New York City area conform to behavioral and linguistic archetypes that are greatly defined by generational parameters. First-generation members of these ethnic groups thus react to the adduced competition and decision-making process as a unit, and so do the second-generation members.

Despite these noticeable differences, Spanish continues to be an integral part of the lives of these communities. It is present, valued, and serves a purpose. The ethnolinguistic vitality of the communities appears to be strong and solid. Cubans, Dominicans, and Puerto Ricans may not receive adequate institutional support, and as cohorts, they may not have the status that others have, but demographically speaking they are powerful enough to overcome these disadvantages and make the presence of the Spanish language obvious.

The idiosyncrasies of New York City have also contributed to these results. Different ethnic groups have been concentrated in well-defined segregated areas and these mini-communities have been able to develop their own ways of surviving and providing services to its members, within its borders and in the mother tongue. These communities have expanded throughout the years and its members have immigrated to other areas in and outside the City. Nevertheless, they continue to be extensions of their homelands for those who share ethnicity with those who are still there, and part of experiencing and embracing this 'homeland outside the homeland' involves using Spanish.

Y. R. Solé's (1980) statements can be perfectly applied to describe the circumstances that have propitiated the success of Cubans, Dominicans, and Puerto Ricans in maintaining and preserving the Spanish language in this City. First, most of the members of these communities feel a personal need to communicate in Spanish in various contexts—even if the manifestation of this need entails going against the demands of the majority group that tries to impose the dominant language. Second, they feel the need to preserve intragroup identification versus the desire to identify with the dominant outgroup. This need appears to be deep-rooted among Cubans,

Dominicans, and Puerto Ricans born in the United States as well. Third, the incongruence between the ingroup and outgroup demands has forced people to take sides and they have sided in favor of the ingroup demands. Therefore, there are intrinsic and extrinsic forces fostering the presence and retention of the ancestral tongue; both the individual and its context play crucial roles in the outcome explored in this investigation.

Finally, it is time for the political and social leaders of this country to understand that the presence of Spanish in New York City and in the entire country need not be interpreted as detrimental or as a menace to national harmony. Languages do coexist in many parts of the world, allowing their speakers to function using more than one code without being a threat. As Fishman (1966b) says, this coexistence of languages serves the national interest, promotes group interests that need not be in conflict with national interests, and enriches individual functioning. When the system does not cultivate the coexistence of various languages, as is the case in this country, the results are extreme. There may be perpetuation of inequality and separation via non-integration into mainstream society, or compliance and assimilation via a complete integration into mainstream society. It is our opinion that Cubans, Dominicans, and Puerto Ricans in New York City— as well as other ethnic groups in other parts of the country—are providing a conciliatory model that needs to be taken into consideration. This model proves that Spanish—and any other language—*can* be part of the lives of those who speak it in the United States.

Questionnaire (Spanish)

Sujeto # _____

Cuestionario

Las respuestas de las siguientes preguntas proveen información importante acerca de su trasfondo y de su conocimiento del español y el inglés. Favor de ser lo más preciso/a y cuidadoso/a posible cuando conteste las preguntas. Gracias por su participación.

Haga un círculo alrededor de la letra correcta o provea la información que se le pide.

1. Grupo étnico
   A. Cubano/a
   B. Dominicano/a
   C. Puertorriqueño/a
   D. Otro -> Favor de especificar _____

2. Sexo
   A. Femenino
   B. Masculino

3. ¿Cuántos años tiene? _____ años

4. ¿Dónde nació?
   A. Cuba -> ¿En qué ciudad/pueblo? _____
   B. República Dominicana -> ¿En qué ciudad/pueblo? _____
   C. Puerto Rico -> ¿En qué ciudad/pueblo? _____
   D. Estados Unidos -> ¿En el área de la ciudad de Nueva York?
      A. Sí -> PASE A LA PREGUNTA # 6
      B. No -> PASE A LA PREGUNTA # 6

5. *Si nació en Cuba, la República Dominicana, o Puerto Rico,* ¿cuántos años (en total) ha vivido en los Estados Unidos? _____ años

6. Aproximadamente, ¿cuántos años (en total) vivió usted en los Estados Unidos desde que nació hasta su cumpleaños número 13? No cuente el tiempo que vivió en otro país. _____ años

7. ¿Dónde nació su *madre biológica*?
    A. Cuba -> ¿En qué ciudad/pueblo? _____
    B. República Dominicana -> ¿En qué ciudad/pueblo? _____
    C. Puerto Rico -> ¿En qué ciudad/pueblo? _____
    D. Estados Unidos -> ¿En el área de la ciudad de Nueva York?
        A. Sí
        B. No -> ¿Dónde? _____

8. ¿Dónde nació su *padre biológico*?
    A. Cuba -> ¿En qué ciudad/pueblo? _____
    B. República Dominicana -> ¿En qué ciudad/pueblo? _____
    C. Puerto Rico -> ¿En qué ciudad/pueblo? _____
    D. Estados Unidos -> ¿En el área de la ciudad de Nueva York?
        A. Sí
        B. No -> ¿Dónde? _____

9. ¿Con quién vivía en su cumpleaños número 13? (puede hacer un círculo alrededor de más de una letra)
    A. Madre biológica
    B. Padre biológico
    C. Madrastra -> ¿Dónde nació ella?
        A. Cuba -> ¿En qué ciudad/pueblo? _____
        B. República Dominicana -> ¿En qué ciudad/pueblo? _____
        C. Puerto Rico -> ¿En qué ciudad/pueblo? _____
        D. Estados Unidos -> ¿En el área de la ciudad de Nueva York?
            A. Sí
            B. No -> ¿Dónde? _____
        E. Otro -> Favor de especificar _____
    D. Padrastro -> ¿Dónde nació él?
        A. Cuba -> ¿En qué ciudad/pueblo? _____
        B. República Dominicana -> ¿En qué ciudad/pueblo? _____
        C. Puerto Rico -> ¿En qué ciudad/pueblo? _____
        D. Estados Unidos -> ¿En el área de la ciudad de Nueva York?
            A. Sí
            B. No -> ¿Dónde? _____
        E. Otro -> Favor de especificar _____

E. Hermana(s)
F. Hermano(s)
G. Abuelo(s)
H. Pariente(s)
I. Otra(s) persona(s) no pariente(s) -> ¿Quién(es)? _____

10. ¿Qué idioma (o idiomas) se hablaba en su casa en su cumpleaños número 13?
    A. Sólo español
    B. Mayormente español
    C. Español e inglés
    D. Mayormente inglés
    E. Sólo inglés

11. ¿Qué idioma (o idiomas) habla usted en su casa ahora?
    A. Sólo español
    B. Mayormente español
    C. Español e inglés
    D. Mayormente inglés
    E. Sólo inglés

12. ¿En qué idioma recibió usted educación formal en la escuela?
    A. Sólo (o mayormente) en español
    B. Sólo (o mayormente) en inglés
    C. Educación bilingüe (español e inglés)
    D. Educación bilingüe y después educación en inglés -> ¿En qué grado estaba cuando empezó a recibir educación sólo en inglés?
       _____ grado
    E. Sólo inglés y después educación bilingüe -> ¿En qué grado estaba cuando empezó a recibir educación bilingüe?
       _____ grado

13. Aproximadamente, ¿cuál es el ingreso económico anual de su actual hogar (antes de que se deduzcan impuestos)?
    $_____ por año

14. ¿Qué nivel de instrucción ha alcanzado?
    A. No tiene diploma de escuela secundaria
    B. Diploma de escuela secundaria o su equivalente (G.E.D.)
    C. Grado Asociado
    D. Algo de educación universitaria (pero sin graduarse)
    E. Diploma de universidad (bachillerato o escuela graduada)
    F. Otro -> Favor de especificar _____

15. ¿Cuántas horas por semana usted pasa . . .
    A. escuchando la radio en *español* o música en *español*?
       _____ horas a la semana
    B. mirando televisión en *español*?
       _____ horas a la semana

16. ¿Con qué frecuencia lee usted periódicos o revistas en *español*?
    A. Diariamente
    B. Varias veces a la semana
    C. Una vez a la semana
    D. Varias veces al mes
    E. Aproximadamente una vez al mes
    F. Menos de una vez al mes
    G. Nunca

17. ¿Cuántas horas por semana usted pasa.
    A. escuchando la radio en *inglés* o música en *inglés*?
       _____ horas a la semana
    B. mirando televisión en *inglés*?
       _____ horas a la semana

18. ¿Con qué frecuencia lee usted periódicos o revistas en *inglés*?
    A. Diariamente
    B. Varias veces a la semana
    C. Una vez a la semana
    D. Varias veces al mes
    E. Aproximadamente una vez al mes
    F. Menos de una vez al mes
    G. Nunca

Para las preguntas 19, 21, 23, 25, y 27–42, haga un círculo alrededor de la letra que indica su respuesta.

19. En su opinión, ¿es necesario saber *hablar español* en el área de la ciudad de Nueva York para mejorar económicamente? (1 = no es nada necesario, 5 = extremadamente necesario)

    No es nada necesario   Es extremadamente necesario

                    1   2   3   4   5

20. Explique su respuesta para la pregunta 19.

_____

_____

_____

_____

21. En su opinión, ¿es necesario saber *hablar inglés* en el área de la ciudad de Nueva York para mejorar económicamente? (1 = no es nada necesario, 5 = extremadamente necesario)

No es nada necesario   Es extremadamente necesario

1   2   3   4   5

22. Explique su respuesta para la pregunta 21.

_____

_____

_____

_____

23. En su opinión, ¿es necesario poder hablar *español* para ser miembro de la comunidad cubana, dominicana o puertorriqueña (el grupo étnico que usted indicó en la pregunta # 1)? (1 = no es nada necesario, 5 = extremadamente necesario)

No es nada necesario   Es extremadamente necesario

1   2   3   4   5

24. Explique su respuesta para la pregunta 23.

_____

_____

_____

_____

25. En su opinión, ¿es necesario poder hablar *español* para ser miembro de la comunidad hispana/latina? (1 = no es nada necesario, 5 = extremadamente necesario)

    No es nada necesario   Es extremadamente necesario

    1   2   3   4   5

26. Explique su respuesta para la pregunta 25.

    _____

    _____

    _____

    _____

27. Evalúe su habilidad para *leer* en español (1 = no sé leer, 5 = sé leer perfectamente)

    No sé leer   Sé leer perfectamente

    1   2   3   4   5

28. Evalúe su habilidad para *leer* en inglés (1 = no sé leer, 5 = sé leer perfectamente)

    No sé leer   Sé leer perfectamente

    1   2   3   4   5

29. Evalúe su habilidad para *escribir* en español (1 = no sé escribir, 5 = sé escribir perfectamente)

    No sé escribir   Sé escribir perfectamente

    1   2   3   4   5

30. Evalúe su habilidad para *escribir* en inglés (1 = no sé escribir, 5 = sé escribir perfectamente)

    No sé escribir   Sé escribir perfectamente

    1   2   3   4   5

31. Evalúe su habilidad para *hablar* en español (1 = no sé hablar, 5 = sé hablar perfectamente)

    No sé hablar   Sé hablar perfectamente

    1   2   3   4   5

32. Evalúe su habilidad para *hablar* en inglés (1 = no sé hablar, 5 = sé hablar perfectamente)

No sé hablar   Sé hablar perfectamente

1   2   3   4   5

33. Evalúe su habilidad para *comprender* español hablado (1 = no comprendo, 5 = comprendo perfectamente)

No comprendo   Comprendo perfectamente

1   2   3   4   5

34. Evalúe su habilidad para *comprender* inglés hablado (1 = no comprendo, 5 = comprendo perfectamente)

No comprendo   Comprendo perfectamente

1   2   3   4   5

35. Compare sus *destrezas generales* en español (ahora) con las de las personas que vivían con usted en su cumpleaños número 13 (1 = mis destrezas son peores, 5 = mis destrezas son mejores)

Peores   Iguales   Mejores

1   2   3   4   5

36. Compare sus *destrezas generales* en inglés (ahora) con las de las personas que vivían con usted en su cumpleaños número 13 (1 = mis destrezas son peores, 5 = mis destrezas son mejores)

Peores   Iguales   Mejores

1   2   3   4   5

37. Compare sus *destrezas generales* en español (ahora) con las de sus hermanos(as), parientes, o amigos cercanos (*del mismo grupo étnico que indicó en la pregunta # 1*) (1 = mis destrezas son peores, 5 = mis destrezas son mejores)

Peores   Iguales   Mejores

1   2   3   4   5

38. Compare sus *destrezas generales* en inglés (ahora) con las de sus hermanos(as), parientes, o amigos cercanos (*del mismo grupo étnico que indicó en la pregunta # 1*) (1 = mis destrezas son peores, 5 = mis destrezas son mejores)

Peores		Iguales		Mejores
1	2	3	4	5

39. Compare sus *destrezas generales* en español (ahora) con las de la mayoría de los miembros de su comunidad (*del mismo grupo étnico que indicó en la pregunta # 1*) (1 = mis destrezas son peores, 5 = mis destrezas son mejores)

Peores		Iguales		Mejores
1	2	3	4	5

40. Compare sus *destrezas generales* en inglés (ahora) con las de la mayoría de los miembros de su comunidad (*del mismo grupo étnico que indicó en la pregunta # 1*) (1 = mis destrezas son peores, 5 = mis destrezas son mejores)

Peores		Iguales		Mejores
1	2	3	4	5

41. Compare sus *destrezas generales* en español (ahora) con las de la mayoría de los miembros de su comunidad (*de otros grupos hispanos/latinos, diferentes al que indicó en la pregunta # 1*) (1 = mis destrezas son peores, 5 = mis destrezas son mejores)

Peores		Iguales		Mejores
1	2	3	4	5

42. Compare sus *destrezas generales* en inglés (ahora) con las de la mayoría de los miembros de su comunidad (*de otros grupos hispanos/latinos, diferentes al que indicó en la pregunta # 1*) (1 = mis destrezas son peores, 5 = mis destrezas son mejores)

Peores		Iguales		Mejores
1	2	3	4	5

43. ¿Hay algo más que pueda añadir sobre sus *destrezas generales* en español? Siéntase en libertad de comentar sobre cosas que no se mencionan en el cuestionario.

_____

_____

_____

_____

44. ¿Hay algo más que pueda añadir sobre sus *destrezas generales* en inglés? Siéntase en libertad de comentar sobre cosas que no se mencionan en el cuestionario.

_____

_____

_____

_____

45. ¿Qué idioma(s) usa *en su trabajo?*
    A. Sólo español
    B. Mayormente español
    C. Español e inglés
    D. Mayormente inglés
    E. Sólo inglés

46. ¿Qué idioma(s) usa *para comunicarse con miembros de su familia?*
    A. Sólo español
    B. Mayormente español
    C. Español e inglés
    D. Mayormente inglés
    E. Sólo inglés

47. ¿Qué idioma(s) usa *para comunicarse con amigos cercanos?*
    A. Sólo español
    B. Mayormente español
    C. Español e inglés
    D. Mayormente inglés
    E. Sólo inglés

48. ¿Qué idioma(s) usa *para comunicarse con otros miembros de su comunidad (del mismo grupo étnico que indicó en la pregunta # 1)*?
    A. Sólo español
    B. Mayormente español
    C. Español e inglés
    D. Mayormente inglés
    E. Sólo inglés

49. ¿Qué idioma(s) usa *para comunicarse con otros miembros de su comunidad (de otros grupos hispanos/latinos, diferentes al que indicó en la pregunta # 1)*?
    A. Sólo español
    B. Mayormente español
    C. Español e inglés
    D. Mayormente inglés
    E. Sólo inglés

Questionnaire (English)

Subject # _____

Questionnaire

The following questions provide important information about your background as well as your knowledge of both Spanish and English. Please be as accurate and thorough as possible when answering the following questions. Thank you for your participation.

Please circle the appropriate letter and/or provide the information requested.

1. Ethnic group
    A. Cuban
    B. Dominican
    C. Puerto Rican
    D. Other -> Please specify _____

2. Sex
    A. Female
    B. Male

3. How old are you? _____ years old

4. Where were you born?
    A. Cuba -> In what city/town? _____
    B. Dominican Republic -> In what city/town? _____
    C. Puerto Rico -> In what city/town? _____
    D. The United States -> In the New York City area?
        A. Yes -> GO TO QUESTION # 6
        B. No -> GO TO QUESTION # 6

5. *If you were born in Cuba, the Dominican Republic, or Puerto Rico,* how many years (in total) have you lived in the United States?____ years

6. About how many years (in total) did you live in the United States between the time you were born and your 13th birthday? Do not count time you lived in another country. _____ years

7. Where was your *biological mother* born?
    A. Cuba -> In what city/town? _____
    B. Dominican Republic -> In what city/town? _____
    C. Puerto Rico -> In what city/town? _____
    D. The United States -> In the New York City area?
        A. Yes
        B. No -> Where? _____

8. Where was your *biological father* born?
    A. Cuba -> In what city/town? _____
    B. Dominican Republic -> In what city/town? _____
    C. Puerto Rico -> In what city/town? _____
    D. The United States -> In the New York City area?
        A. Yes
        B. No -> Where? _____

9. Who did you live with on your 13th birthday? (you may circle more than one letter)
    A. Biological mother
    B. Biological father
    C. Stepmother -> Where was she born?
        A. Cuba -> In what city/town? _____
        B. Dominican Republic -> In what city/town? _____
        C. Puerto Rico -> In what city/town? _____
        D. The United States -> In the New York City area?
            A. Yes
            B. No -> Where? _____
        E. Other -> Please specify _____
    D. Stepfather -> Where was he born?
        A. Cuba -> In what city/town? _____
        B. Dominican Republic -> In what city/town? _____
        C. Puerto Rico -> In what city/town? _____
        D. The United States -> In the New York City area?
            A. Yes
            B. No -> Where? _____
        E. Other -> Please specify _____

E. Sister(s)
F. Brother(s)
G. Grandparent(s)
H. Relative(s)
I. Other non-relatives -> Who? _____

10. What was the language (or languages) spoken at home on your 13th birthday?
    A. Spanish only
    B. Mostly Spanish
    C. Both Spanish and English
    D. Mostly English
    E. English only

11. What language (or languages) do you speak at home now?
    A. Spanish only
    B. Mostly Spanish
    C. Both Spanish and English
    D. Mostly English
    E. English only

12. In what language did you receive formal instruction in school?
    A. Spanish only
    B. English only
    C. Bilingual education (both Spanish and English)
    D. Bilingual education and then English only -> What grade were you in when you were transferred to an English only classroom?
       _____ grade
    E. English only and then bilingual education -> What grade were you in when you were transferred to a bilingual education classroom?
       _____ grade

13. Approximately, what is the annual income in your present household (before taxes are taken out)?
    $_____ per year

14. What is your education level?
    A. No high school diploma
    B. High school diploma or G.E.D.
    C. Associate Degree
    D. Some college education (but did not graduate)
    E. College diploma (B.A. or graduate school)
    F. Other -> Please specify _____

15. How many hours per week do you spend . . .
    A. listening to *Spanish-language* radio or *Spanish* music?
       _____ hours per week
    B. watching *Spanish-language* television?
       _____ hours per week

16. How often do you read *Spanish* newspapers or magazines?
    A. Daily
    B. Several times a week
    C. Once a week
    D. Several times a month
    E. About once a month
    F. Less than once a month
    G. Never

17. How many hours per week do you spend.
    A. listening to *English-language* radio or *English* music?
       _____ hours per week
    B. watching *English-language* television?
       _____ hours per week

18. How often do you read *English* newspapers or magazines?
    A. Daily
    B. Several times a week
    C. Once a week
    D. Several times a month
    E. About once a month
    F. Less than once a month
    G. Never

For questions 19, 21, 23, 25, and 27–42, please circle the number of your response.

19. In your opinion, how necessary is it to be able to speak *Spanish* in the New York City area to get ahead economically? (1 = not necessary at all, 5 = extremely necessary)

    Not necessary at all   Extremely necessary

               1   2   3   4   5

20. Explain your response to question 19.

_____

_____

_____

_____

21. In your opinion, how necessary is it to be able to speak *English* in the New York City area to get ahead? (1 = not necessary at all, 5 = extremely necessary)

Not necessary at all   Extremely necessary

             1   2   3   4   5

22. Explain your response to question 21.

_____

_____

_____

_____

23. In your opinion, how necessary is it to be able to speak *Spanish* to be a member of the Cuban, Dominican, or Puerto Rican community (the ethnic group you indicated on question # 1)? (1 = not necessary at all, 5 = extremely necessary)

Not necessary at all   Extremely necessary

             1   2   3   4   5

24. Explain your response to question 23.

_____

_____

_____

_____

25. In your opinion, how necessary is it to be able to speak *Spanish* to be a member of the Hispanic/Latino community? (1 = not necessary at all, 5 = extremely necessary)

Not necessary at all   Extremely necessary

    1   2   3   4   5

26. Explain your response to question 25.

_____

_____

_____

_____

27. Rate your Spanish *reading* ability (1 = cannot read in Spanish, 5 = can read perfectly in Spanish)

Cannot read   Can read perfectly

    1   2   3   4   5

28. Rate your English *reading* ability (1 = cannot read in English, 5 = can read perfectly in English)

Cannot read   Can read perfectly

    1   2   3   4   5

29. Rate your Spanish *writing* ability (1 = cannot write in Spanish, 5 = can write perfectly in Spanish)

Cannot write   Can write perfectly

    1   2   3   4   5

30. Rate your English *writing* ability (1 = cannot write in English, 5 = can write perfectly in English)

Cannot write   Can write perfectly

    1   2   3   4   5

31. Rate your Spanish *speaking ability* (1 = cannot speak Spanish, 5 = can speak Spanish perfectly)

Cannot speak   Can speak perfectly

    1   2   3   4   5

32. Rate your English *speaking ability* (1 = cannot speak English, 5 = can speak English perfectly)

Cannot speak   Can speak perfectly

          1   2   3   4   5

33. Rate your ability to *understand spoken* Spanish (1 = cannot understand at all, 5 = can understand perfectly)

Cannot understand   Can understand perfectly

          1   2   3   4   5

34. Rate your ability to *understand spoken* English (1 = cannot understand at all, 5 = can understand perfectly)

Cannot understand   Can understand perfectly

          1   2   3   4   5

35. Rate your current overall Spanish *language skills* compared to those of the adults who lived with you on your 13th birthday (1 = my skills are worse, 5 = my skills are better)

          Worse   Same   Better

          1   2   3   4   5

36. Rate your current overall English *language skills* compared to those of the adults who lived with you on your 13th birthday (1 = my skills are worse, 5 = my skills are better)

          Worse   Same   Better

          1   2   3   4   5

37. Rate your current overall Spanish *language skills* compared to those of your siblings, relatives, or closest friends (*from the same ethnic background, as you indicated on question # 1*) (1 = my skills are worse, 5 = my skills are better)

          Worse   Same   Better

          1   2   3   4   5

38. Rate your current overall English *language skills* compared to those of your siblings, relatives, or closest friends (*from the same ethnic background, as you indicated on question # 1*) (1 = my skills are worse, 5 = my skills are better)

Worse		Same		Better
1	2	3	4	5

39. Rate your current overall Spanish *language skills* compared to those of the majority of the members of your community (*from the same ethnic background, as you indicated on question # 1*) (1 = my skills are worse, 5 = my skills are better)

Worse		Same		Better
1	2	3	4	5

40. Rate your current overall English *language skills* compared to those of the majority of the members of your community (*from the same ethnic background, as you indicated on question # 1*) (1 = my skills are worse, 5 = my skills are better)

Worse		Same		Better
1	2	3	4	5

41. Rate your current overall Spanish *language skills* compared to those of the majority of the members of your community (*from other Hispanic/Latino backgrounds, different from the one you indicated on question # 1*) (1 = my skills are worse, 5 = my skills are better)

Worse		Same		Better
1	2	3	4	5

42. Rate your current overall English *language skills* compared to those of the majority of the members of your community (*from other Hispanic/Latino backgrounds, different from the one you indicated on question # 1*) (1 = my skills are worse, 5 = my skills are better)

Worse		Same		Better
1	2	3	4	5

43. Is there anything else about your Spanish *language skills* that you would like to comment on? Please feel free to make comments about things which were not covered on this questionnaire.

_____

_____

_____

_____

44. Is there anything else about your English *language skills* that you would like to comment on? Please feel free to make comments about things which were not covered on this questionnaire.

_____

_____

_____

_____

45. What language(s) do you use *on your job*?
    A. Spanish only
    B. Mostly Spanish
    C. Both Spanish and English
    D. Mostly English
    E. English only

46. What language(s) do you use *to communicate with family members*?
    A. Spanish only
    B. Mostly Spanish
    C. Both Spanish and English
    D. Mostly English
    E. English only

47. What language(s) do you use *to communicate with close friends*?
    A. Spanish only
    B. Mostly Spanish
    C. Both Spanish and English
    D. Mostly English
    E. English only

48. What language(s) do you use *to communicate with other members of your community (from the same ethnic background, as you indicated on question # 1)?*
    A. Spanish only
    B. Mostly Spanish
    C. Both Spanish and English
    D. Mostly English
    E. English only

49. What language(s) do you use *to communicate with other members of your community (from other Hispanic/Latino groups, different from the one you indicated on question # 1)?*
    A. Spanish only
    B. Mostly Spanish
    C. Both Spanish and English
    D. Mostly English
    E. English only

Notes

NOTES TO CHAPTER THREE

1. Question 13 was not used in this study. It deals with the annual income of the present household and most subjects were not willing to provide this information.
2. The analysis for generation and ethnic group was only conducted for the phonemes /-r/ and /-s/ because these were the only phonemes that applied to the three dialects.

NOTES TO CHAPTER FOUR

1. Alternative F ('Other') was selected by only a handful of subjects, and those who selected it specified that they had completed graduate studies, possibility that was included in alternative E. We changed their answers to alternative E.
2. Alternatives C and D were erroneously switched on the questionnaire. This was corrected before the data were analyzed.
3. Since the answers provided in the questionnaire by the subjects were in hours per week, a six-point scale was created in order to conduct the statistical analysis: 1 = 0–5 hours per week, 2 = 6–10 hours per week, 3 = 11–15 hours per week, 4 = 16–20 hours per week, 5 = 21–25 hours per week, and 6 = more than 25 hours per week.
4. For this discussion we reassigned meanings to the values in the five-point scale: 1 = No skills, 2 = Poor skills, 3 = Average skills, 4 = Good skills, 5 = Excellent skills. These meanings stay in tune with the values used in the questionnaire. (See Appendices.)

Bibliography

Alba, O. "Estudio socioligüístico de la variación de las líquidas finales de palabra en el español cibaeño." In *Studies in Caribbean Spanish Dialectology*, edited by R. M. Hammond and C. Resnick. Washington, DC: Georgetown University Press, 1988.

Amastae, J., and L. Elías-Olivares, L., eds. *Spanish in the United States: Sociolinguistic Aspects.* New York: Cambridge University Press, 1982.

Attinasi, J. "Language attitudes in a Puerto Rican community." In *Bilingual Education and Public Policy in the United States,* edited by R. V. Padilla. Ypsilanti, MI: Eastern Michigan University, 1979.

Bailey, D. J. "Status of the Hispanic population in the United States." In *The Hispanic Population of the United States: An Overview.* Congressional Research Service, Subcommittee on Census and Population. Washington, DC: Government Printing Office, 1983.

Bean, F. D., and M. Tienda, M. *The Hispanic Population of the United States.* New York: Russell Sage Foundation 1987.

Bergen, J., ed. *Spanish in the United States: Sociolinguistic Issues.* Washington DC: Georgetown University Press, 1990.

Bloomfield, L. *Language.* New York: Henry Holt, 1933.

Elerik, C. "On the form of bilingual grammars: The phonological component." In *A Festschrift for Jacob Ornstein: Studies in General Linguistics and Sociolinguistics,* edited by E. L. Blansitt, Jr. and R. V. Teschner. Rowley, MA: Newbury House, 1980.

Elías-Olivares, L., E. A. Leone, R. Cisneros, and J. R. Gutiérrez, eds. *Spanish Language Use and Public Life in the USA.* Berlin: Mouton, 1985.

Fishman, J. A. 1964. Language maintenance and language shift as a field of inquiry: A definition of the field and suggestions for its further development. *Linguistics* 9: 32–70.

_____. "Language maintenance in a supra-ethnic age: Summary and conclusions. In *Language Loyalty in the United States,* edited by J. A. Fishman, V. C. Nahirny, J. E. Hoffman, and R. G. Hayden. The Netherlands: Mouton, 1966a.

_____. "Planned reinforcement of language maintenance in the United States: Suggestions for the conservation of a neglected national resource." In *Language Loyalty in the United States,* edited by J. A. Fishman, V. C. Nahirny, J. E. Hoffman, and R. G. Hayden. The Netherlands: Mouton, 1966b.

121

_____. "The relationship between micro- and macro-sociolinguistics in the study of who speaks what language to whom and when." In *Bilingualism in the Barrio*. Vol. 7, *Language Science Monographs*, edited by J. A. Fishman, R. L. Cooper, and R. Ma. Bloomington: Indiana University Press, 1971.

_____. 1984. Mother tongue claiming in the United States since 1960:Trends and correlates related to the "revival of ethnicity." *International Journal of the Sociology of Language* 50: 21–99.

Floyd, M. B. "Spanish in the Southwest: Language maintenance or shift?"In *Spanish Language Use and Public Life in the USA*, edited by L. Elías-Olivares, E. A. Leone, R. Cisneros, and J. R. Gutiérrez. Berlin: Mouton, 1985.

Gans, H. J. 1992. Second-generation decline: Scenarios for the economic andethnic futures of the post-1965 American immigrants. *Ethnic and Racial Studies* 15: 173–92.

García, O. "Spanish language loss as a determinant of income among Latinos in the United States: Implications for language policy in schools." In *Power and Inequality in Language Education*, edited by J. W. Tollefson. New York: Cambridge University Press, 1995.

García, O., I. Evangelista, M. Martínez, C. Disla, and B. Paulino. 1988. Spanish language use and attitudes: A study of two New York City communities. *Language in Society* 17: 475–511.

Glazer, N. "The process and problems of language-maintenance: An integrative review." In *Language Loyalty in the United States*, edited by J. A. Fishman, V. C. Nahirny, J. E. Hoffman, and R. G. Hayden. The Netherlands: Mouton, 1966.

Grasmuck, S., and R. Grosfoguel. 1997. Geopolitics, economic niches, and gendered social capital among recent Caribbean immigrants in New York City. *Sociological Perspectives* 40: 339–63.

Greenfield, L., and J. A. Fishman. "Situational measures of normative language views of person, place and topic among Puerto Rican bilinguals." In *Bilingualism in the Barrio*. Vol. 7, *Language Science Monographs,* edited by J. A. Fishman, R. L. Cooper, and R. Ma. Bloomington: Indiana University Press, 1971.

Guitart, J. M. "A propósito del español de Cuba y Puerto Rico: hacia un modelo no sociolingüístico de lo sociodialectal." In *Corrientes actuales en la dialectología del Caribe hispánico*, edited by H. López Morales. San Juan, PR: Editorial Universitaria de la Universidad de Puerto Rico, 1978.

_____. "Conservative versus radical dialects in Spanish: Implications for language instruction. In *Bilingual Education for Hispanic Students in the United States*, edited by J. A. Fishman and G. D. Keller. New York: Teachers College Press, 1982a.

_____. 1982b. On the use of the Spanish subjunctive among Spanish-English bilinguals. *Word* 33: 59–67.

_____. "Spanish in contact with itself and the phonological characterization of conservative and radical styles." In *Spanish in Contact: Issues in Bilingualism*, edited by A. Roca and J. B. Jensen. Boston: Cascadilla Press, 1996.

Gumperz, J. J. *Language in Social Groups*. Stanford, CT: Stanford University Press, 1971.

Gutiérrez, M. "Sobre el mantenimiento de las cláusulas subordinadas en el español de Los Angeles." In *Spanish in the United States: Sociolinguistic Issues*, edited by J. J. Bergen. Washington, DC: Georgetown University Press, 1990.

Gynan, S. N. "La nueva política en los Estados Unidos: Propósitos y motivos." In *Language and language use: Studies in Spanish*, edited by T. A. Morgan, J. F. Lee, and B. VanPatten. New York: University Press of America, 1987.

Hamers, J. F., and M. H. Blanc. *Bilinguality and Bilingualism*. Cambridge: Cambridge University Press, 1989.

Hart-González, L., and M. Feingold. 1990. Retention of Spanish in the home. *International Journal of the Sociology of Language* 84: 5–34.

Hayden, R. G. "Some community dynamics of language maintenance." In *Language Loyalty in the United States*, edited by J. A. Fishman, V. C. Nahirny, J. E. Hoffman, and R. G. Hayden. The Netherlands: Mouton, 1966.

Hidalgo, M. "The dialectics of Spanish language loyalty and maintenance on the U.S.-Mexico border: A two generation study." In *Spanish in the United States: Linguistic Contact and Diversity*, edited by A. Roca, and J. M. Lipski. Berlin: Mouton de Gruyter, 1993.

Hoffman, G. "Puerto Ricans in New York: A language-related ethnographic summary." In *Bilingualism in the Barrio*. Vol. 7, *Language Science Monographs*, edited by J. A. Fishman, R. L. Cooper, and R. Ma. Bloomington: Indiana University Press, 1971.

Holmes, J. *Learning About Language: An Introduction toSociolinguistics*. New York: Longman, 1994.

Hudson-Edwards, A., and G. D. Bills. "Intergenerational language shift in an Albuquerque barrio." In *A Festschrift for Jacob Ornstein: Studies in General Linguistics and Sociolinguistics*, edited by E. L. Blansitt, Jr., and R. V. Teschner. Rowley, MA: Newbury House, 1980.

Jacobson, R. "The social implications of intra-sentential code-switching." In *Spanish in the United States: Sociolinguistics Aspects*, edited by J. Amastae and L. Elías-Olivares. New York: Cambridge University Press, 1982.

Jensen L., and Y. Chitose. 1994. Today's second generation: Evidence from the1990 U.S. Census. *International Migration Review* 28: 714–35.

Jiménez Sabater, M. A. "Estructuras morfosintácticas en el español dominicano: algunas implicaciones sociolingüísticas." In *Corrientes actuales en la dialectología del Caribe hispánico*, edited by H. López Morales. San Juan, PR: Editorial Universitaria de la Universidad de Puerto Rico, 1978.

Klee, C. A. "Differential language usage patterns by males and females in a rural community in the Rio Grande Valley." In *Language and Language Use: Studies in Spanish*, edited by T. A. Morgan, J. F. Lee, and B. VanPatten. New York: University Press of America, 1987.

Klee, C., and L. Ramos-García. (1991). *Sociolinguistics of the Spanish-Speaking World*. Tempe, AZ: Bilingual Press, 1991.

Labov, W. *Social Stratification of English in New York City*. Arlington, VA: Center for Applied Linguistics, 1966.

_____. *Sociolinguistic Patterns*. Philadelphia: University of Pennsylvania Press, 1972.

_____. "Field Method of the Project on linguistic change and variation." In *Language in Use*, edited by J. Baugh and J. Sherzer. Englewood Cliffs, NJ: Prentice Hall, 1984.

Labov, W. and P. Pedraza, P. *A study of the Puerto Rican speech community in New York City*. Report to the Urban Center of Columbia University, 1971.

Lipski, J. M. *Latin American Spanish*. New York: Longman, 1994.

López, D. 1982. Chicano language loyalty in an urban setting. *Sociology and Social Research* 62: 167–78.

López Morales, H. "Más allá de la regla variable: la velarización de /r/ en el español de Puerto Rico." In *Language and Language Use: Studies in Spanish*, edited by T. A. Morgan, J. F. Lee, and B. VanPatten. New York: University Press of America, 1987.

Matluck, J. H. "Bilingualism of Mexican-American children: Language characteristics." In *A Festschrift for Jacob Ornstein: Studies in General Linguistics and Sociolinguistics*, edited by L. Blansitt, Jr., and R. V. Teschner. Rowley, MA: Newbury House, 1980.

Milán, W. G. "Spanish in the inner city: Puerto Rican speech in New York." In *Bilingual Education for Hispanic Students in the United States*, edited by J. A. Fishman, and G. D. Keller. New York: Teachers College Press, 1982.

Milroy, L. "Social network and linguistic focusing. In *Sociolinguistic Variation in Speech Communities*, edited by S. Romaine. London: Arnold, 1982.

_____. (1987). *Language and Social Networks*. 2nd ed. Oxford: Basil Blackwell, 1987.

Ocampo, F. "El subjuntivo en tres generaciones de hablantes bilingües." In *Spanish in the United States: Sociolinguistic Issues*, edited by J. J. Bergen. Washington, DC: Georgetown University Press, 1990.

Oropesa, R. S., and N. S. Landale. 1997. In search of the new second generation: Alternative strategies for identifying second generation children and understanding their acquisition of English. *Sociological Perspectives* 40: 429–55.

Otheguy, R., and O. García. "Convergent conceptualizations as predictors of degree of contact in U.S. Spanish." In *Spanish in the United States: Linguistic Contact and Diversity*, edited by A. Roca and J. M. Lipski. Berlin: Mouton de Gruyter, 1993.

Padilla, A. M., and K. J. Lindholm. "Development of interrogative, negative, and possessive forms in the speech of young Spanish / English bilinguals." In *Bilingual Education for Hispanic Students in the United States*, edited by J. A. Fishman and G. D. Keller. New York: Teachers College Press, 1982.

Pedraza, P. "Language maintenance among New York Puerto Ricans." In *Spanish Language Use and Public Life in the USA*, edited by L. Elías-Olivares, E. A. Leone, R. Cisneros, and J. R. Gutiérrez. Berlin: Mouton, 1985.

Pérez, L. 1994. The household structure of second-generation children: An exploratory study of extended family arrangements. *International Migration Review* 28: 736–47.

Pfaff, C. W. "Constraints on language-mixing: Intrasentential code-switching and borrowing in Spanish / English." In *Spanish in the United States: Sociolinguistics Aspects*, edited by J. Amastae and L. Elías-Olivares. New York: Cambridge University Press, 1982.

Poplack, S. '"Sometimes I'll start a sentence in Spanish *y termino en español*": Toward a typology of code-switching.' In *Spanish in the United States: Sociolinguistics Aspects*, edited by J. Amastae and L. Elías-Olivares. New York: Cambridge University Press, 1982.

Portes, A., and R. G. Rumbaut. *Immigrant America: A Portrait*. Berkeley,CA: University of California Press, 1996.

Portes, A., and R. Schauffler. 1994. Language and the second generation: Bilingualism yesterday and today. *International Migration Review* 28: 640–61.

Roca, A., and J. M. Lipski, eds. *Spanish in the United States: Linguistic Contact and Diversity*. Berlin: Mouton de Gruyuter, 1993.

Roca, A., and J. B. Jensen, eds. *Spanish in Contact: Issues in Bilingualism*. Somerville, MA: Cascadilla Press, 1996.

Romaine, S. *Bilingualism*. Oxford: Blackwell, 1995.

Rumbaut, R. G. "Ties that bind: Immigration and immigration families in the United States." In *International Migration and Family Change*, edited by A. Booth, A. C. Crouter, and N. Landale. New York: Lawrence Earlbaum, 1997.

Sánchez, R. "Our linguistic and social context." In *Spanish in the United States: Sociolinguistics Aspects*, edited by J. Amastae and L. Elías-Olivares. New York: Cambridge University Press, 1982.

Silva-Corvalán, C. "Algunos aspectos de la gramática de los niños bilingües de Los Angeles, Estados Unidos." In *Bilingüismo y adquisición del español*, edited by H. Urrutia Cárdenas and C. Silva-Corvalán. Bilbao, Spain: Instituto Horizonte, SL, 1992.

_____. *Language Contact and Change: Spanish in Los Angeles*. Oxford: Clarendon Press, 1994.

_____. *Spanish in Four Continents: Studies in Language Contact and Bilingualism*. Washington, DC: Georgetown University Press, 1995.

Sobin, N. "On transference and inversion." In *A Festschrift for Jacob Ornstein: Studies in General Linguistics and Sociolinguistics*, edited by E. L. Blansitt, Jr., and R. V. Teschner. Rowley, MA: Newbury House, 1980.

Solé, C. A. "Language usage patterns among a young generation of Cuban-Americans." In *A Festschrift for Jacob Ornstein: Studies in General Linguistics and Sociolinguistics*, edited by E. L. Blansitt, Jr., and R. V. Teschner. Rowley, MA: Newbury House, 1980.

_____. "Language loyalty and language attitudes among Cuban-Americans." In *Bilingual Education for Hispanic Students in the United States*, edited by J. A. Fishman and G. D. Keller. New York: Teachers College Press, 1982.

Solé, Y. R. "The Spanish / English contact situation in the Southwest." In *A Festschrift for Jacob Ornstein: Studies in General Linguistics and Sociolinguistics*, edited by E. L. Blansitt, Jr., and R. V. Teschner. Rowley, MA: Newbury House, 1980.

_____. "La difusión del español entre mexicano-americanos, puertorriqueños y cubano-americanos en los Estados Unidos." In *Language and language use: Studies in Spanish*, edited by T. A. Morgan, J. F. Lee, and B. VanPatten. New York: University Press of America, 1987.

_____. 1990. Bilingualism: Stable or transitional? The case of Spanish in the United States. *International Journal of the Sociology of Language* 84: 35–80.

Stone, G. B. "Language choice among Mexican-American high-school students in Saint Paul, Minnesota: Some preliminary findings." In *Language and Language Use: Studies in Spanish,* edited by T. A. Morgan, J. F. Lee, and B. VanPatten. New York: University Press of America, 1987.

U.S. Bureau of the Census. *The Hispanic Population: Census 2000 Brief.* Prepared by B. Guzmán for the U.S. Department of Commerce, Economics and Statistics Administration, Bureau of the Census. Washington, DC, 2001. http://www.census.gov/prod/2001pubs/c2kbr01–3.pdf.

U.S. Bureau of the Census. *The Hispanic Population in the United States: March 2002.* Prepared by R. R. Ramírez and G. P. de la Cruz for the U.S. Department of Commerce, Economics and Statistics Administration, Bureau of the Census. Washington, DC, 2003. http://www.census.gov/prod/2003pubs/p20–545.pdf.

Valdés, G. "Social interaction and code-switching patterns: A case study of Spanish/English alternation." In *Spanish in the United States: Sociolinguistics Aspects,* edited by J. Amastae and L. Elías-Olivares. New York: Cambridge University Press, 1982.

Veltman, C. *Language Shift in the United States.* Berlin: Mouton, 1983.

_____. 1988. Modeling the language shift process of Hispanic immigrants. *International Migration Review* 22: 545–62.

_____. 1990. The status of the Spanish language in the United States at the beginning of the 21st century. *International Migration Review* 24: 108–23.

Wald, B. 1987. Spanish-English grammatical contact in Los Angeles: The grammar of reported speech in the East Los Angeles English contact vernacular. *Linguistics* 25: 53–80.

Wolfram, W. *Overlapping influence in the English of second generation Puerto Rican Teenagers in Harlem.* Arlington, VA: Center for Applied Linguistics, 1971.

Zentella, A. C. 1982. Spanish and English in contact in the United States: The Puerto Rican experience. *Word* 33: 41–57.

_____. "El impacto de la realidad socio-económica en las comunidades hispanoparlantes de los Estados Unidos: Reto a la teoría y metodología lingüística." In *Spanish in the United States: Sociolinguistic Issues,* edited by J. J. Bergen. Washington, DC: Georgetown University Press, 1990a.

_____. 1990b. Lexical leveling in four New York City Spanish dialects: Linguistic and social factors. *Hispania* 73: 1094–1105.

_____. 1990c. Returned migration, language, and identity: Puerto Rican bilinguals in dos worlds / two mundos. *International Journal of the Sociology of Language* 84: 81–100.

Index

Printed in the United States
by Baker & Taylor Publisher Services